Returning to Work

A guide to re-entering the job market

2nd edition

Sally Longson

howtobooks

Published by
How To Books Ltd, 3 Newtec Place,
Magdalen Road, Oxford OX4 1RE, United Kingdom
Tel: 01865 793806 Fax: 01865 248780

First edition 1999
Second edition 2002

British Library Cataloguing in Publication Data
A catalogue record for this book is available from
the British Library

Cover design by Baseline Arts Ltd, Oxford

Produced for How To Books by Deer Park Productions
Typeset by PDQ Typesetting, Stoke-on-Trent, Staffs.
Printed and bound in Great Britain

Note: The material contained in this book is set out in good
faith for general guidance and no liability can be accepted for
loss or expenses incurred as a result of relying in particular circumstances on statements made in
the book. The laws and regulations are complex and liable to change, and readers
should check the current position with the relevant
authorities before making personal arrangements.

Contents

Preface

After you've been at home for a while, it's easy to forget that you have skills and qualities to offer. For many, the thought of returning to the workplace becomes increasingly fraught with potential problems. There can be a tendency to put it off. 'Well, maybe after the children have left secondary school/ university/got married/had children.'

But the idea of going back to work is also an intriguing one, and there are plenty of positive reasons to do it: to raise your self-esteem; to enhance your own personal development; to be seen as an individual rather than as somebody's wife, partner or mother, or even daughter; to acquire new skills and confidence; and to go out into the workplace to seek new adventures. More practically, in a world where job security is a thing of the past, it's not a bad idea to have two incomes in a household.

We'll all probably need to work for longer – perhaps until we're 70 – to boost our pension funds, but not at a constant 'nine-to-five, four weeks' holiday a year' rate. People are more likely to acquire paid employment as they need to, dipping in and out of the workplace. Already employers are increasingly used to people changing career and having periods of employment, training, study and travel. There's more help out there for those seeking to run their own businesses or who've been out of work for some time, whatever the reason. This is all good news for you, the woman returning to work. Employers aren't put off by people who've taken breaks, and there's lots of help about for people who want to retrain and change from one way of life to another.

This book wants to focus on you, but it recognises that dependants such as children and elderly relatives can play their part in affecting the opportunities open to you. Although this book does not deal with the subject of childcare in detail, it gives tips throughout on how to handle your dependants and your responsibilities to them, together with details of organisations you can contact for more help.

On a personal note, I would like to thank my husband, Paul, for his enthusiastic support throughout; my parents, family and friends for their interest, especially my mother who tried out many of the exercises in this book; and everyone at How To Books for their willingness to entrust me with this project.

Finally, remember the words of the writer, Tennyson:

Come my friends
'Tis not too late to seek a newer world.

Sally Longson

CHAPTER 1

Moving On

L ife is like a book, containing a series of chapters which all link together and eventually have a life story to tell. Some chapters are straightforward while others – especially those involving careers, marriages and motherhood – offer more of a challenge. You manage to juggle your relatives, your partner and friends on the one hand, and dirty nappies, Playdoh and muddy PE kit in the other. Inevitably, each chapter of your life draws to a conclusion and a new one dawns.

Recognising it's time to move on

If you've picked up this book, then you're ready to start a new chapter in your life, rather like Jane, in the case study below.

Case study: Jane, a mother of three _____

It's a funny thing, raising children. You bring them up, wanting them to be independent, able to stand on their own two feet in this world, and to be happy and loved. And yet, when they finally leave, it is *so hard*. You just have to smile, wave them off, and keep the tears to yourself later, when they've gone. You know that you're moving on to another phase of your own life and that it's time to go on to something else. _____

Why change now?

Something has sparked you off to decide it's time to make a change. Maybe the kids have gone off to university, or are taking their gap year, or have found a job and moved out. Perhaps you just want to do something different with your life, to earn money of your own, to fulfil a dream or fuel an interest, or to increase your self-confidence and prove to yourself that you can cope. Or a friend has returned to the workplace or even gone out to work for the first time – and tickled your interest, and you wonder: 'How would I fare in the workplace? What would I do? What could I achieve?'

Whatever your reasons for picking up this book, it will help you move on to a new chapter in your life.

Knowing when it's time to move is a skill

In fact, it is a *vital* skill in work today. Many people stay in the same old job, wondering why they are becoming increasingly frustrated and uninterested in what they are doing. Unless they make a determined effort to change their lot, the danger is that things will only get worse, as Figure 1 illustrates, and as you may find for yourself, as you begin to realise that you want to make changes to your life.

You think, 'I'm so *bored*.'

↓

You have feelings of frustration and lack of interest,
loss of concentration and pride.
Your self-esteem falls.

↓

You're less effective in your work –
things get slack – your 'things to do' list gets longer.

↓

You starting ringing in sick, turning up late and leaving early
– routine tasks become increasingly cumbersome and take longer to do.

↓

The boss notes your lack of interest and enthusiasm
and the family notice you whinging and whining.

↓

You get warnings about your performance and attitudes
and meet them with a 'What do I care' response;
your partner asks what's wrong and you can't be bothered to tell him.

↓

You're fired! Your confidence gets lower.
You can't be bothered to do anything.

Fig. 1. Knowing when it's time to move on.

Many of us don't listen to ourselves saying 'move' because we don't believe it's our responsibility to change our situation or perhaps it's simply easier to stay put as we are. Perhaps, too, we fear making that change for its consequences, preferring the apparent 'security' we have at present. Our failure to take action to change our situation leads to more frustration and pent-up anger within ourselves.

> **You've recognised that you need to move on and that you have to do something about it. Congratulate yourself.**

Moving on takes effort

As women, we know that when we want something to happen *we* have to make it happen. The ironing won't do itself – it's up to us to get on with it. The same is true for job hunting: it takes motivation to get out there and find a job.

> **Remember – women excel at making things happen.**

When that ready effort is laced with nerves or thoughts of 'what if?', the tendency is to put off doing anything. For many of us, the thought of going through the job-hunting process and then starting work is very nerve-racking. But thousands of women go back to work every year. After the initial plunge into unknown waters, they find it's much less difficult to swim than they thought it would be, although it's not easy. It takes some juggling to combine domestic responsibilities with work and deal with the stereotypical attitudes that still exist. But, nonetheless, it can be done. And now it's your turn. This book will show you how to get there.

It's never too late

People change their careers every day all over the country. Some work already and want to do something different, perhaps to start up their own business or to move from a commercial environment into a more caring one. Others may have been made redundant or sacked and forced to rethink their lives and what they want from a career. Some want to go out to work after raising a family and/or running a house.

You're not alone in wanting to change your career – or your life.

Many people change careers because they are bored or they want to expand their job horizons. Samantha trained to be a physiotherapist and, after practising for several years, became a biology teacher instead. Helena moved from nursing into journalism. Others want greater security, such as the gardener who wants a less physically demanding job as he gets older.

'I want to change my lifestyle'

Some seek a complete lifestyle change, like the City banker seeking to get away from the rat race and the stress, who moves into the country to take up a different occupation. Then there's the serviceman who has travelled continually throughout his career, working in one location then uprooting to another. He's had enough and leaves the services to find work which allows him to spend more time at home with his family.

The change is possible these days because the avenues open to train for different careers are increasing all the time. There are more ways 'in' than there were before. In fact, most of us will have four, five or even six career changes in our working lifetime.

Don't be an 'if only' statistic

Think about the number of times you've heard people say, 'I'd love to do something different' or 'I'd love to do something with animals' or whatever it is they want. I can think of two straightaway and both worked for a bank. Their lives took off when one trained to become a commercial pilot and the other became an air traffic controller. They took the chance and made the break. *They made it happen – training and all – through their own efforts.* You can, as well.

Be prepared to train

Even if you were already working, the probability is that you would need to train or re-train to change your career. There are no excuses *not* to learn. We live in an 'any place, any time' society, which means you can learn to do practically anything at your own pace at home, in your public library, at the local college or adult education centre, or in Internet cafes. On-line learning, backed by practical sessions to help you put theory into practice, means that changing to a new career has become far more feasible. And, if your study skills are rusty or your IT skills non-existent, there are courses for people returning to study to help you gingerly step back into it, however confident you are about your ability to cope.

> **It's not too late to start learning. You can still do it.**

Study gives you the chance to make a fresh start; it provides you with a new interest after the kids have left home. Your confidence will rocket as you prove to yourself you can do it. Furthermore, recent studies show an employer that you are able and willing to learn and (especially if the course is related to the sort of work you want to do) are up to date. The government's commitment to lifelong learning reflects the importance of keeping abreast of change and the need to keep learning throughout life. Nor are you restricted to studying the traditional subjects such as History, English Literature or Science. There's an exciting range of subjects available throughout the country, many of which are related to specific career sectors, such as counselling, care courses, public relations, horticulture ... the list is endless.

Just two more things: adult education is *very* different from your school days. And adult students make very good students. Why? Because they are *committed* to learning. And people are getting better at learning because there are more ways *to* learn, so you can choose the method which suits you best.

Employers need your skills and qualities

On the one hand, there are fewer school leavers than there used to be. Employers have been affected by demographic changes and many young people are choosing to remain in full time education. So employers are looking elsewhere to recruit staff, and one avenue open to them is that of women returners.

On the other hand, the nature of today's workplace demands many of the skills and qualities more mature people, and particularly women, have.

Take the example of Alison, below. Like her, you've probably continued at some stage to direct operations in the house even when you're sick:

Case study: Alison _____

I had a terrible stomach upset last week – but I still had to run the house, even from my bed. The kids kept coming in and asking me to settle arguments, what to cook and for how long, and whinging that there was no clean PE kit for school. It was chaotic and I got no peace . . . I got up in the end. _____

Alison is showing skills which can be used at work:
- leading others and running the place
- negotiating to keep everyone happy
- sharing her knowledge with others
- demonstrating stamina and commitment which enables her to get things done and to keep going.

Understanding what employers want

Some employers need to recruit staff with specific qualifications, knowledge and experience because of the job the employee will be doing. But every employer will also want to get what is described as the 'culture fit' right; that is, will the applicant fit in well with the rest of the team? Employers will look for someone who can add particular qualities to a team. They will also want to recruit people with the right attitude: those who are committed to learning, who will go the extra mile to provide customer service and who will help ensure that the customer comes back again and again.

Employers seek people with the right attitude and qualities – recruiting staff is not normally about finding the brainiest person in Britain. After all, if you were to recruit a cleaner, you'd want them to be thorough, reliable and honest, wouldn't you? You wouldn't ask prospective recruits if they had a degree.

Mature people are in demand

Many employers want to recruit people who can offer a mature, reliable approach; and who are committed to what they are doing.

Case study: Gavin, Hairdresser _____

I wanted a receptionist who would really welcome people, offer them tea or coffee, show them to a seat, make appointments, answer the telephone – that sort of thing. I took a few young people on, because I wanted to give them a chance. But many turned up for a couple of days and didn't bother coming in after that. Now I've got a lady called Suki in her 40s, who is wonderful. She is totally reliable, superb with the customers – warm and interested in them – and I know I can get on with what I should be doing because I don't have to worry about her. _____

Mature people offer qualities which employers will welcome, such as accuracy, reliability, motivation, enthusiasm and pride in what they're doing. In an increasing number of service industries, the way in which customers are welcomed and helped is of increasing importance and will enhance or destroy customer loyalty.

Some stores are beginning to target older people. ASDA is one of these, B&Q another. They both believe in giving people a second chance. Stores such as these want people with maturity and experience who will offer high quality customer service. Mature people have had the experience of developing a number of skills in organising themselves, managing people and thinking ahead – as we will see in Chapter 5.

> **Mature people have experience of life.**

Women have more opportunities now

Huge numbers of women are working and succeeding at their jobs. Women make excellent managers, leaders and team players.

- More women are achieving:
  - professional qualifications
  - public recognition
  - board directorships
  - success in their own businesses
  - managerial levels.
- Women are more likely to work flexitime, and are less likely to be unemployed on a long-term basis than men.

◆ Women dominate jobs in health, education and public administration.

Consider how the following points can actually work to a woman's advantage:

1   You don't have to look for a nine-to-five job – working hours are far more flexible. Many banks for example are offering people contract hours for 20 to 25 hours a week to cover their busiest times.

2   A host of IT developments and a plethora of careers enable increasing numbers of people to work from home – useful if you have an elderly relative who needs care, thus making it hard for you to leave the house.

3   Academic qualifications are not enough on their own to ensure success in job hunting. Your ability to network, present yourself and plan your move back are the keys to success.

There are more careers to choose from

The workplace has been transformed over the centuries by several revolutions, including the printing press, the agrarian revolution, the industrial revolution and, in our own times, the technological and communications revolution. New careers have resulted from them all – and world events, changes in social attitudes and legislation have enabled men and women to take advantage of them all.

Along with changing social attitudes, each revolution has added to the range of jobs available. Science, technology, and an increasing emphasis on personal satisfaction, growth and development have resulted in a huge expansion of careers. Look at the pet industry: there are now canine beauticians, pet counsellors, animal therapists and dieticians, as well as dog trainers, animal behaviourists (who specialise), pet breeders, pet portrait painters and dog walkers. Animal rescue centres and charities abound, from international to local concerns. They all need staff with different abilities and skills – but all with a concern for the welfare of animals. And this list does not even begin to mention the more traditional careers with animals such as vets, pet shop owners and assistants, kennel assistants and stable hands.

This book will help you establish what sort of job would interest you – and then show you how to get it while remaining on speaking terms with your loved ones and maintaining your sanity.

Your attitude counts, not your years

Even back in 1998, the *Mail on Sunday* in July 1998, quoted 50 success stories of women all earning over £1 million a year. They included writers, TV presenters, fitness gurus, a TV cook, pop-singers and entertainers – and business women. Some names are household ones: Nicola Horlick, and Carol Galley in finance and Anita Roddick of the Body Shop. The most successful mentioned in the *Mail on Sunday*, Mary Dodson, has a Bristol-based company which she began in her garage with £500.

You may read that paragraph and have a number of reactions:

◆ 'I'd love to do that.'
◆ 'Oh, well, dream on.'
◆ 'It's all very well for her ...'
◆ 'I wonder how she did it?'
◆ 'Another woman who's made it big. I don't want to make it big. I just want to get out of this house and do something different.'

> You can do it – whatever 'it' is. You don't have to be an Einstein to get a job you enjoy.

Everyone has their own career aspirations. Some, like Carol, are happy with where they are now:

Case study: Carol, Specialist Teaching Assistant _____

I love my job as a specialist teaching assistant. I really think my experience with my own kids has given me something extra to offer, especially as the class teacher is new to teaching this term. I thought about teacher training, but seeing all the paperwork she has to contend with and the extra study it would involve ... no, I'm happy as I am. My reward is seeing the kids' happy faces when they've done well. You can't beat that. _____

Others want more from their job. Andrea returned to a sales position, because she'd done it before she had her family. But this time, she decided to take her career further and a talk with the personnel department enabled her to join a management development programme at the local college. She now manages a team of six.

Jennifer's husband had left her after 18 years of marriage. She explains why she went out to work:

Case study: Jennifer, Library Assistant _____

I never thought I'd cope. My confidence took such a bashing after Rob left me – he'd told me for so long how useless I was at anything. I just wanted to prove to myself that I wasn't, to find some self-respect. Plus I needed the cash. At work, everyone really appreciates my help. My confidence is growing all the time and the money is coming in. Life is slowly getting better. _____

The workplace is still fun

Work can still be fun, despite all the talk about pressure and targets. In many organisations staff take advantage of their employer's resources in ways they shouldn't. They spend hours advising what Susie should do with her boyfriend; they use the telephone to organise their social lives, book a holiday, and shout at the bank. They use the fax machine to confirm hotel reservations. Friendships are made, affairs had, hearts broken. People go to work for the companionship as much as anything else; too many leave work on a Friday night knowing that the next time they have a really social conversation will be when they get back to work on Monday morning.

Everyone has the same sorts of worries. Throughout the country, staff are saying to each other, 'My son wants a new bike for Christmas, goodness knows how we're going to pay for it' or 'Did you see *Coronation Street* last night? What do you think will happen next?'

Taking control of your career

Take time to think about:

◆ what you want to do
◆ where you want to work – the environment, what sort of workmates etc.

- why you want a job
- when you want to work and how long for
- how you and your partner will cope with the household chores.

Finally, remember that job hunting will take time if you want to find the right job for you.

> **The more you take control of your own future and know what you want, the more likely you are to get it.**

This book will help you make these decisions and, hopefully, end up with a lifestyle that suits and pleases you.

Try it now

- Analyse the way you spend your time during two typical weeks. Note down anything which takes up your time. Later, you'll analyse those activities for the skills you need to do them.
- Read the local and national papers for information about careers, running your own business and women returning to the workplace. Is there anything which interests you?
- Talk to three people you know who work. How have their career aspirations changed since starting work? Ask them to describe a typical working day. Does any of it appeal?

Summary

Congratulate yourself; you've taken the first steps in moving your life forward on to another stage.

- Remember, changing careers is far from unusual today.
- What you make of your career is up to you – you're in the driving seat.
- Remember that because of demographic changes and the need for more mature abilities and skills, employers are looking for new sources of staff.

*Decide how
your job will
fit into your
lifestyle*

CHAPTER 2

Considering Your Lifestyle

T his chapter will help you think about where a job might
fit into your life. After all, life is not just about working.
Everybody has their own idea of 'the perfect life'; at the least,
most of us would like to have time to spend with family,
nurturing children, getting the bills paid, having fun with
friends and generally enjoying life.

As you work through the exercises and questions in this
chapter, use them as things to think about as you proceed in
your efforts to find work. As you research the opportunities
open to you, the needs and wishes you pinpoint here may
change, but an early focus on what is important will help in
your job hunting.

What do you want from life?

A job is only a part of your life. Greater flexibility in working
hours means that you don't have to look for a nine-to-five job,
five days of the week. You may want to combine your domestic
responsibilities with a job which is part-time and fits in with
the rest of your life, so you will need to decide how much time
such a job will take up. This is something you will need to
discuss with your family.

For many women, thinking about our own needs is not
easy. Our schooling and upbringing has taught us to think of
others first. If we are used to pleasing others all the time, it is
more difficult for us to know what we want for ourselves –
we're so used to thinking of everybody else.

> **It's time to please yourself and think about what you want
> in your life.**

Life is not a dress rehearsal – this is it

This is your time to work out what *you* want to do in the future that will fulfil *you* and bring *you* enjoyment and satisfaction. You now need to analyse your life and work out what you want to do more of, what you want to get rid of, either through delegating the task or eliminating it altogether, and what you want to introduce. This chapter will help you do this and work out where a job fits into your life, based on your own needs and lifestyle.

Working the hours you want

Look through your local paper and a national paper. List as many different hours as you can to see what employers are looking for. Why would they need to recruit staff for these hours?

We live in an 'any time, anywhere' society. An increasing number of services operate around the clock already, such as:

hospitals	fire services
police	armed forces
veterinary medicine	banks
financial services	supermarkets
home services such as plumbers	the media
travel industry	hair and beauty services
education and training	hospitality industry
IT specialists	secretarial services

This 'any time, anywhere' society is changing the way many companies employ staff, because they need to keep going around the clock.

Technology has made a difference

Technological developments mean that you don't have to work at the same place every day any more. The busy executive can work in his or her hotel room, on an aircraft or from home. Employees may come into work each day and sit down at the first desk they see in a large room of terminals. Many people now work from home, only going into the office for meetings or 'to keep in touch' or to hear about new projects and to get training.

Organisations are cutting costs

To make the most efficient use of their resources, employers are recruiting fewer people on a permanent, full-time basis. Instead, they recruit core staff such as managers and specialists who are responsible for the direction of the business. They employ other staff for short periods of time as they are needed. When the busy time is over, the staff are let go. If there's going to be a heavy workload for two or three months because they've taken on a project for a client, then they'll take staff on for a contract of two or three months until that project is over. This enables the company to respond to unpredictable but instant customer demands. As a result, many posts are offered on a temporary, contract and part-time basis.

> **Employers need a more flexible workforce.**

In an attempt to encourage women back to work, more employers are offering schemes such as career breaks, retainer schemes, re-entry schemes and parental leave. (This is partly for good public relations within the community.) Here are some examples of the sort of posts on offer:

◆ June works as a secretary in a school, term time only (some holiday cover is required before the start and after the end of each term).

◆ Nashilla works as a finance clerk in a recruitment agency Monday, Tuesday and Wednesday. On Thursday and Friday, her friend Samantha takes over. They both share the post and in fact applied for the post as a partnership, having already worked out when they would each work.

◆ Mandy is a freelance beauty therapist.

◆ Joanna works on a contract basis: she is coming to the end of a six-month contract and has been asked to stay on, but she is more excited about an opportunity with a building society which will give her two years' work.

◆ Annette has agreed to work for 1,620 hours every year with a clearing bank. She will work out with her supervisor when those hours are to be put in, but expects to work at the bank's busiest times, such as lunch hours.

◆ Sandra is a life-coach: she works from home, mostly in the evenings, coaching people who want to set and achieve goals and make the most of their lives.

◆ Toyah is a temporary nanny employed by an agency – she fills in for nannies who are sick or on holiday. She may work a full week one week, and a couple of days the next, depending on how busy her agency is and how many days she wants to work.

This doesn't all work like magic. There will always be conflicts to be resolved between the needs of the business and its employees, not just in terms of the customers' demands but also friction between those at work *with* dependants (be they elderly or young) and those *without*. Not every company will offer adequate working conditions; their web-sites and careers literature will give you an indication of how far they go. The good news is that the government introduced new rights for part-time workers in July 2001, so, for example, they now have the same access to company pension schemes and the same hourly rates as their full-time colleagues.

Contract and temporary work

Many skilled people are contracted by an employer or agency to work for a specified time agreed at the beginning of a contract and to fulfil a specific role and responsibility.

On this basis, you would:

◆ gain wide experience of different companies and cultures
◆ expand your range of skills and competencies
◆ get a reference from each employer if you've done a good job
◆ increase your network of contacts, thereby enhancing your job opportunities – word of mouth is a common recruitment method
◆ work the hours and time to suit you (up to a point)
◆ possibly be offered a permanent post.

But on the other hand you might:

◆ find yourself without work (and money) between assignments
◆ grow tired of the continual change, especially if you're temping
◆ find yourself without holidays or sick pay – check the

position before you start.

A portfolio worker may have two or three sorts of jobs, which together make up a full-time working week. For example, you could work for a care home two days a week *and* work in a office for three. If you should be made redundant from one job, you still have the other. But you do need to be organised, taking into account time and cost of travel between jobs and home, and whether a change of clothes is necessary to suit the culture of each firm.

What are you looking for?

The job you have and the number of hours you work may depend on why you're going to work and what else you want to achieve within your life.

Case study: Nicole, a mother and housewife _____

I loved doing my voluntary work and didn't want to give it up, but I also wanted to prove to myself I could get a job and keep it. So I decided to work part time so that I could continue to do my voluntary work. _____

Others go back because they have no choice. That doesn't mean they don't have a right to a job they enjoy and colleagues they respect and look forward to working with.

Case study: Michelle needed the money _____

I *had* to go back, I needed the money. I couldn't imagine anyone taking me on, because Graham had made me feel such a failure. Seventeen years of being told how useless you are, by the man who supposedly loves you, has a terrible effect on your self-esteem. But I had to get myself sorted out – I needed the cash, because he left me virtually nothing, and it was quite a battle to get anything off him. I had no choice – I had to work full time. _____

Linda stayed at home to raise her four children while Bob worked, and planned to spend most of her time with him when he retired. But then he died suddenly of a heart attack after he had finished work. 'It was such a shock', Linda said, 'that I couldn't bear being at home alone all day, so I now work full time in a day care centre for elderly people. The money helps, of course, but it's the friendship I really go for.'

What about you?

Ask yourself why you want to go back. Here are some of the reasons people return to work – do any of them apply to you? How important are they? Add any other reasons of your own that you can think of, then try scoring each of them according to whether you think they are Essential/Important/Nice to have/ Not at all important. This will help you determine what you're looking for and what is important to you. As you proceed through your search for the right job, some of these reasons may change in importance as your ideas about your future ideal job shift.

◆ the extra cash
◆ money – I have no choice
◆ the challenge
◆ to meet new people
◆ to socialise
◆ to travel
◆ to see how far I can get in my career
◆ to get out of the house
◆ to be creative
◆ to run my own business
◆ to have fun
◆ to meet someone
◆ to gain some independence.

Look down your list. You may be able to achieve some of these needs by means other than finding a part-time job, such as:

◆ joining an adult education course or doing a correspondence course
◆ getting involved in voluntary work
◆ taking up a new hobby or interest.

Explore all your options so that you can decide what is best for you and be in a better position to plot and explain your return to the workplace.

Establishing some basic needs

We all have our own needs and views on what we want out of life. Here are some questions to ask yourself as you proceed with your job search:

How many hours to work?

Do you want to work full time or part time? If part time, how many hours a week? Does it matter when those hours are?

Part-time workers *are* often paid less than full-time – substantially so in some sectors. On the other hand, the time away from work can be used to get further qualifications or study for another sort of job just while the cash is coming in, or the kids are going through their final years at home. If you do end up with a low-paid, part-time position in which you feel you are a slave, aim to work your way out of it. Build on any experience you can get, show ambition, ask about company training schemes which may be relevant, get further qualifications and look for areas of work and companies where you will be better rewarded after acquiring experience. In fact, a recent survey showed that those working part time were more likely to be promoted than those working *full* time. If nothing happens, move to another job where your potential will be recognised and your ambitions respected and fulfilled.

How quickly do you need a job?

If you need a job quickly because of your financial situation, visit your Job Centre and sign on; an adviser will discuss your options with you, show you the vacancy boards and give you information about any relevant training programmes and any benefits to which you might be entitled. Try not to apply for the first job you see: a bit of thought about what you want may mean that you achieve greater happiness and success at work. At the least, a part-time job would give you time to train for a career while keeping the money coming in.

If you have any financial commitments which must be honoured, such as a mortgage, explain your family's current predicament to the lender so that together you can work out a repayment plan acceptable to both sides. This will help to reduce the pressure on your job hunting. Prepare an interview outfit so that you can respond quickly to invitations to an interview. And remember, you still have a right to enjoy working – most people do, however much they moan about it when their week starts!

Do you want a job or a career?

A job is a task to be done, executed, undertaken. It is usually a short-term thing, although some people can have jobs for years, but the word 'job' doesn't take with it the idea of a journey, progression and ambition as the 'career' does. A career is long term, building on a series of stepping stones. Which appeals to you the most? Of course, a job can develop into a career.

Do you want to go back to your previous job?

Although this may look like the obvious option if you have worked before, you should ask key questions, such as: Does your previous job still exist? Does the company still exist? If not, what has replaced it? Would you still want the same level of responsibility as you had before, for example? Or more? Or less? Have your views on what constitutes the right job for you changed in the time you have been at home?

How much training are you willing to do?

How much training are you prepared to do as a springboard to a job? A ten-week course? One year? None at all? What impact will training have on your job prospects and what sort of learning to do you want to do? Do you want to do an academic course which will leave your options open and could take up to three years' full-time study? Or a ten-week course designed to give you an extra skill at speed to offer an employer? These are all questions you need to think about.

How much responsibility do you want?

There are pros and cons of having responsibility:

Low	High
Less money	More money
In and out, no need to think about the job at home once you have left work	You may take it home with you – either literally or in your thoughts. You may be on 24-hour call.
Day-to-day vision of the job	Tendency to think about the future of the organisation and your career
May supervise small number of staff	May supervise many staff
More routine work	Less routine
Less say in the direction of the company	More say in the direction of the company
More contact with customers	Less contact with customers

Here are two lists of jobs, each paired off. Compare the level of responsibility they have.

nurse	doctor
teacher	headmistress
secretary	manager
probation officer	social worker
waitress	hotel manager
retail manager	checkout operator
nanny	cleaner
mechanical engineer	aeronautical engineer

Of the above pairs, who has the most contact with customers. Which would you prefer?

Think about yourself

Which level of responsibility appeals to you more? The more you have, the more that job may overlap into other areas of your life (i.e. your time for leisure). Of course, you may enjoy the responsibility so much that you don't mind!

Do you actively seek responsibility? Can you give three examples of times you took on responsibility and how you handled them? Did you enjoy them? Why? Did you wish you could have taken on more? Why?

Making changes to your lifestyle

Consider your life as it is now. Ask yourself the following
questions:

◆ How will you cope with all your domestic responsibilities,
your leisure activities *and* working, taking into account the
number of hours you would like to work?

◆ Of the activities you listed from Try it now on page 11,
what would happen if each one were ignored, done less
frequently, or not done at all? Could somebody else do it?

◆ Are there any practicalities you need to solve if you go out
to work (such as, who would do your elderly mother's
shopping) which might otherwise prevent you from working
full time?

◆ Do you want to continue, add to or get rid of for the
change, any of your current leisure pursuits and voluntary
activities? Do you have any 'friends' you spend time with
but you'd welcome an excuse to see less of?

◆ What is important to you in the future as your family
(including elderly relatives) get older?

If you delete from your life things that you want to leave
behind, like leisure activities you are bored with or friends you
have outgrown, then you create more time for yourself.

Keeping your options open

In thinking about the way a job might fit into your lifestyle,
allow some flexibility in your planning. After working for a few
months, you may have a number of different reactions to being
at work:

◆ 'I'm happy doing this for a while. It suits me and my needs
at home; I like my work colleagues and they seem to be
pleased I'm here. And it's got me out of the house, which
was the main reason I wanted to work.'

◆ 'I could run this sort of business on my own. I wonder
whether I could set up my own company? We could turn
the garage into an office.'

◆ 'I wonder how much more responsibility I could handle? I'd

love to find out!'
- ◆ 'I don't want any more responsibility than this. It suits me fine. It means I can still do the other things I want, like my tennis, and work with the RSPCA.'
- ◆ 'I wonder whether I'll still be doing this next year?'

Your aspirations and plans will alter as your experiences and circumstances change. Be open to opportunity and be prepared to let some things go for a while or even forever.

Considering the impact of a job

It's not just being *at work* that makes the difference, but the time it takes getting ready for work, thinking about it, socialising with people from work, deciding what to wear for it, not to mention getting there! It will probably take up more time than you think it will.

A job will change your life.

Don't forget that you should have time to renew your energy when you're tired and to regain your peace when you're fed up with people. I relish my time when I get lost in reading about gardens ... Each to their own! Allow time for you!

What is vital to your lifestyle?

Think about those things you *won't* compromise over. We're not as flexible as we like to think we are! What would you guard particularly carefully in your life? What would you want to make sure you had time for? There may be leisure activities or voluntary work you're currently doing and want to continue, for example. How much time do you need for these? Take a sheet of paper and rank the following in order of importance to you. Are the ones at the bottom of your ranking *that* important to you or could you either spend less time on them than before; or not do them at all?
- ◆ time to spend with your partner
- ◆ time to spend with your parents/partners' parents
- ◆ time to spend with your kids
- ◆ time to spend with your pets

- time to spend with friends
- opportunity to travel
- a job/career
- your own business
- opportunity to spoil yourself
- taking up something you've never tried before
- chance to make new friends
- chance to make up for lost education
- developing yourself further
- good health
- exercise
- looking after the house
- looking after the garden.

This will help you decide where a job fits in – and how much pressure you want within it.

Try it now

- Consider how many hours you would like to devote to each of the activities which are important to you in a week.
- Write down what action you need to take to make sure this happens (apart from getting a job), such as delegating more of your chores, sharing more responsibilities with your partner/children.
- Work out who will be affected by these changes.

Summary

You need to think about your whole lifestyle to make sure that you will be happy with your lot when you start work.

1 Tell yourself it's okay to delegate. What's the worst that can happen if somebody else does the housework?

2 If you're worried about losing control over a job you've done for years in the house, remind yourself what you're going to do with the time and the money instead.

3 Everyone will reach a stage in their current role when they know it's time to move on. Look back at what you've achieved with pride and move forward.

CHAPTER 3

Dealing with Barriers

Returning to work is fraught with barriers for many women, not the least of which may be family resistance to the idea and our own lack of self-confidence. But we all have more strength and courage within us than we think. Recognise your barriers and develop strategies for dealing with them. Think of the times you've told your children, 'You can do it,' and yes, they have; and you always knew *they would*. Put some of the faith you have in them into yourself.

First, here is some ammunition for you to fire at your loved ones (or anyone else) who thinks your place is – still – in the home.

Living in challenging times

In the last century it was degrading for a married woman to take paid employment, because to do so implied that her husband couldn't provide for her. How times have changed! Paid employment – even occasional part-time work – will be increasingly important to *everybody* owing to:

- ◆ lack of job security – how would your family cope if your partner or husband was suddenly made redundant? So he says he won't be? How does he know?
- ◆ divorce and separation – people are more likely to end up on their own;
- ◆ financial responsibilities ahead – university fees for the children, taking care of your parents, your own retirement fund;
- ◆ the need to pay for a particular thing, e.g. a new car, school fees, that special holiday.

As the number of elderly people are growing, it is going to become harder for the State to keep everybody in their old age. We'll all have to do more to look after ourselves without State help in every aspect of our lives. Put your toe back in the job market now. Take control and build up reserves of cash and self-reliance so that you're in a stronger position to cope with the unexpected, and able to enjoy life more, later on.

Coping with well-meaning relatives

'Brilliant idea! How can we help?' Some relatives will be delighted when you tell them you're going out to work. They will support you, offer advice, look out for the right job for you, call you to say they've seen an advertisement for a job that would suit you down to the ground and drive you to the interview on the day. If this sounds like yours, you're lucky. Other readers won't have such supportive families or partners and an airing of their wish to go back to work might be met with, 'You're going back to work? *Why?*'

Case study: Sam, Mortgage Adviser

My mother-in-law couldn't understand *why* I was going out to work. 'Doesn't Roger work hard enough for you?' she kept asking me – right in front of him, too, which was embarrassing. She thought it was all about money. In a way, it was – I wanted to earn something myself, but I also wanted time to spend on me, to do something for myself and to see if I would cope at work. I tried to ignore remarks – but it was hard. I really had to bite my tongue at times. It was certainly worth the effort in the end. Now that I'm actually working and she can see how much I'm enjoying it, she's finally shut up.

Do they understand what you're doing?

Even more annoying is the person who refuses to take you seriously when you tell them you're going back to work. Don't let them put you off by saying things like, 'You're far too old to go back to work!' Ignore them, don't let them put you down. You are *not* too old to be going back to work.

When they start being negative about your job prospects, ask yourself how much they really know about the job market, how much research they have done into it and on what facts their opinions are founded.

Example

According to your mother/husband, Mrs Foggatt from Number 38 has spent six months looking for a job – and has failed to find one. Your relatives are probably assuming that there are no jobs out there for people of Mrs Foggatt's age (similar to yours) or experience. They also suggest that if Mrs Foggatt can't get a job, why would you get one? This makes you think, 'Oh well, perhaps I won't bother. Maybe I'll just leave it for now.'

But ask yourself how much your relatives actually know about:

◆ the way Mrs Foggatt sold herself to prospective employers
◆ how hard she really tried to find a job
◆ whether she researched *every* route into the workplace – did she investigate training programmes for example?
◆ how far she targeted her search at companies which tended to employ women returners
◆ her determination to get a job.

They probably wouldn't have a *clue*.

> It's the process of job hunting and the attitude you take towards it that makes the difference as to whether you're successful or not.

You need people around you who are going to support you and give you confidence, not those who are probably envious or who have different values and needs in life. Yours are just as important as theirs. When the negative people see you're serious – and ultimately successful – they'll soon shut up.

'What about us and our needs?'

Perhaps you've spent a lot of time helping out with other people's children over the holidays (especially if they are working and you are not) and now they wonder how they will ever cope without you. Well, you have a right to work; you've helped out all these years and they are going to have to recognise that you want to do something for yourself now. Suggest solutions to their problems so that you can at least help them out in finding answers. Don't be blackmailed into turning back. It's not fair on you and you'll end up being resentful.

Coping with elderly relatives

The problem with elderly relatives is that it is difficult to know how much longer they will be alive and what their health will be like as they get older. There are no given timescales as there are with children: with children, you know that they will probably be in school until they are 16 or 18 years old and then they may leave home or at least they should be fully independent. But, as we all know, both youngsters and elderly relatives can suddenly become as demanding and unpredictable as each other in terms of the sort of support they need from you.

If you are coping with elderly relatives, find out as much as you can about the help which is available to you both on a day-to-day basis and in the event of an emergency in both the public *and* private sectors. Ask your local Citizens Advice Bureau, the Social Services Department and your family GP for advice; the Department of Social Services has a web-site with information on it for carers. Know exactly what sort of help you can rely on from outside agencies and your own network, what sort of notice they will all need and how much they will cost. You may need to alter your own plans slightly to fit in with your family's initially, at least while you get back into the workplace and until you've proved yourself to an employer. You could, in that time, work from home or start to build up your skills by correspondence courses.

Dealing with friends who envy you

Friends who are negative about your plans may simply envy you! Try asking them, 'Haven't you ever thought of doing something like this, too? I bet you have!' Make light of it – and see what their response is. Offer them the chance to look through your leaflets from the local library or college – they may secretly be longing to have a go, but may be even more afraid than you were when you first started out on your journey to find a job.

> Don't let negative people get you down. You have a right to do what you want to do.

Turn their negatives into pluses

Ask your negative friends whether they know of people who are working whatever their age – and where. They could be a mine of information.

Discussing plans with your partner

The support of your partner will make life much easier. Many men are very supportive of their partners who choose to work and they may even offer helpful suggestions. Talk through your goals with your husband/partner, and don't let him manipulate you into doing something you don't really want just because it's more convenient to him.

Unfortunately, some men may have problems understanding why their partners suddenly want to go out to work after spending so long looking after them and the children. They resent the fact that you want to earn money, feeling that you are undermining their efforts or subconsciously telling them that they aren't doing enough. Perhaps they fear change – especially in you. This can, of course, happen whether you're at work or studying, as Caroline found out:

Case study: Caroline and Mike _____

Mike didn't seem to mind when I signed up for an Access course at the local college. I studied during the day when he was out – he's always worked very long hours, anyway. But when we went on holiday together eight months after I'd started my studies, it made us realise how much I'd changed and how far apart we'd grown. We finally spoke about it after a massive row – we talked one night until four in the morning to try to decide how to resolve our problems and get back the old relationship we once had.

Now we spend time together every weekend to talk and do something different on our own, without the kids. We never do an activity like going to the cinema – it's always something which will get us talking, like going out to dinner or for a walk. Slowly, things are improving, which is a relief – I wasn't going to give up my studies! Actually, I don't think we'll ever go back to our old relationship because I've moved on too much for that – but we have a new and very exciting one. _____

Some reasons why men object to women returning to work

1 He likes you as you are and the thought of you changing terrifies him.
So change together. Get him to do something new, too.

2 He likes to have control over you.
He's dangerous and manipulative, then. He should respect you for what you want to do.

3 He fears you going off to have an affair – will you like the boss more than him? (Recently I spoke to three secretaries in one office, all of whom admitted to having called their male bosses 'darling' by mistake.)
Show him he's the one for you.

4 He is worried you won't need him any more.
Tell him how you need him.

5 He wonders who will do the household chores.
Sit down as a family and work through how you'll get it all done.

6 Who will look after his parents? And the children?
Again, find a solution as a family. You're all involved in this change together.

7 He thinks you've got enough to do with all the housework, shopping, gardening, washing etc.
Get someone to cover the main problem – a cleaner or a gardener. Create a job for somebody else if you can afford to.

8 He worries that his career will be upset.
Unlikely. Remember, his job is important to him too. Can he do any further study or training to increase his chances of being promoted/remaining in work/getting more satisfaction from what he's doing?

9 He likes being the main breadwinner.
So what's wrong with extra back-up?

10 He doesn't want you to have any money of your own beyond what he gives you.
He's a control freak! Some drastic change is needed in your relationship.

Coping with your partner's fears

Explain what the extra money will mean to you as a family. Draw up a mental list of the financial benefits the family might enjoy – eating out, extra short holidays, more exotic long ones. Reassure your partner that you still love him and he's the man for you. Buy him small presents with your new-found earnings, make love more often, ask him for hugs and kisses to show that you still need him, get some sexy underwear, have a romantic evening in. Show him he's still important to you.

Money talks. So talk money.

Always talk things through

If you have a good marriage, your husband is unlikely to mind your going out to work at all. If you are having problems, he may see your ambitions as a sign of the relationship's vulnerability. You may need to get counselling.

Case study: Tracey, whose husband Stuart didn't want her to return to work: _____

Stuart was dead against me going back. We rowed for days. In the end, I sat down with him and pointed out that, for 18 years, I had kept the house for him, looked after his children and his mother for the last three, walked the dog, done all the shopping and provided the taxi service for the kids. Now that the last child has left home, I said to him, I deserve to do something I want to do for me at last. I asked him how he would feel in my position. I also told him that I wanted to spend more time with him now that the children were gone – that helped a lot, because it boosted his esteem, knowing that I wanted to be with him. Finally, he saw it my way. _____

Tell your partner how you're feeling and give him a chance to tell you what he thinks. Difficult, I know, because we all know that men aren't the best communicators – it's far easier for many men to disappear down the pub, turn on the soccer or even go out to wash the car than it is for them to discuss how they feel. Be sure of what you want – and be firm.

And if none of these things work, offer something he may be hard pushed to refuse.

Encourage him to change direction

Perhaps one of the reasons your partner is being so difficult about your doing something new and exciting with your life is that *he* too wants to change his career but has never thought of it before, or didn't dare try while he was the only breadwinner. If there are two of you bringing in the cash, there will be more scope for *him* to have a change of direction as well. Well, why not? Ask him whether he has ever wanted to change career. This may enable him to understand why you want to change your role – and it may provide him with an exciting new direction. If you are both working, this lessens the financial risk of his changing careers.

Handling your children

'Good for you, mum!' Many youngsters will be fully supportive of mum going out to work; you're 'doing your own thing' which makes you happy. Explain how it will affect them. It never does kids any harm to see mum or dad studying and boosting their skills or doing something different.

Get them involved

If your children are still at home while you're going back to work, delegate as many responsibilities as you can to them, within reason and without impinging on their schoolwork. Ask them to help with the housework; praise them regularly and thank them for their efforts. And if it's not up to your standards – so what? What's the worst that can happen?

Make sure you can still give them support

You may still feel that you want to have someone at home if you have kids at home and this may particularly be the case if your children are doing important exams, such as GCSEs or A Levels. You could:

- do part-time work – perhaps mornings only, allowing you to be there in the afternoons to welcome them home from school with a tasty snack;
- try to recruit someone who can be there for them when

they arrive home to see that they sit down to their homework and have something to eat – a college student might be the answer. Get a reference or two, however, before agreeing to take them on;

◆ postpone your return until such a time as their important exams – GCSEs and further education – has passed and start gaining skills in the meantime through adult education, voluntary work etc.

In reality, many children will actually enjoy the independence afforded to them when they arrive home. It's good preparation for when they move away.

Overcoming a lack of confidence

Courses at your local college may help you get back into practice in terms of meeting people, putting your own view forward in a group, and developing skills you'll need at work. These may include:

◆ self-awareness and assertion skills
◆ understanding and handling fear
◆ handling stress
◆ positive thinking
◆ improving your image, style and colour analysis.

These classes will improve your confidence and self-esteem; you'll also meet new friends and get back into a social environment.

Update your study skills

If you are thinking of going back to college, courses on how to study and exam techniques may help. These may include topics such as:

◆ broad-based study skills
◆ preparing assignments and writing essays
◆ preparing for exams
◆ giving presentations
◆ using information technology
◆ time management.

Why not sign up for a course in a subject that you're naturally interested in? You may know a good deal about it already – but that will increase your confidence and interest in the class and any nerves will soon pass. Similarly, you could try something you've always wanted to have a go at – it could lead to a new hobby or even your own business!

Examples include:

flower arranging	fencing
cake decoration	clothes making
ecology and conservation	a language
aromatherapy	upholstery
calligraphy	antiques

But these are merely a few examples of courses on offer – get a prospectus from your local college or library.

The Workers Educational Association (WEA) is a voluntary adult education organisation providing over 10,000 courses every year for over 150,000 students. It runs courses with local universities and adult education colleges in subjects covering history, writing, theatre, bird watching etc. Some courses may enable you to start acquiring credits towards a degree. For more information, see Useful Addresses.

> **Get advice. There are plenty of people ready to help.**

Courses for women returners

Most colleges offer courses specifically for women seeking to return to the workplace, designed to boost confidence and set goals, to prepare a CV and give the chance to practise interviewing skills. They will help connect you with other college courses you might want to follow which are relevant to the workplace. Many courses now include a period of work experience with a sympathetic employer, usually in an area of work which interests you as a future career or job choice. Students on courses for women returners won't be school leavers, but rather women like yourself who are probably in the same situation as you may well be. Your local Job Centre may also offer courses designed to boost your job hunting skills.

You can also see an adviser at a local careers service (this may be a private company and you may have to pay) or local college to discuss your career plans. It is very useful to have somebody impartial to brainstorm your ideas with.

Get some exercise!

This can boost your confidence and motivation. You don't have to take part in team sports; an aerobics course or afternoon cycle will soon make you feel as though you could take on the world. It will also be something to put on your CV as a sign you take your health and fitness seriously and that, as a result, you're unlikely to be absent from work through illness.

Believe in yourself

You can read all the self-help books in the library and attend all the courses available in your area, but what you need to do is to pinpoint what the underlying reason is for your lack of confidence and then find a way to overcome it. Doing the skills audit in Chapter 5 will help boost your self-esteem as you realise, working through the exercises there, that you do have skills and qualities which will be relevant to the workplace. And don't forget that you've spent years keeping abreast of anything and everything which might affect your family and home, so *you know* that you can keep learning.

You may be able to get credit towards qualifications such as NVQs for some of the skills you have acquired in your life through the Accreditation of Prior Learning system (APL). Chapter 9 will expand on this in more detail.

Feeling out of touch

'It's ages since I worked!' It may have been a long time since you worked for an employer which may be very nerve-wracking when you are thinking about going back. You may never have worked as an employee at all. Later on, this book gives some hints on finding out how the workplace has changed and how you can get to grips with the technology and terminology.

When you're talking to people about your plans, there are the few who'll say to you, 'Well, you don't know anything about business life, you haven't been there.' This particular line may come from your partner, family or friends and businessmen – *men* – themselves. It does nothing for your confidence, but you don't have to listen to this sort of comment. Unfortunately, male prejudice does still exist, even if only on a subconscious level.

> **Find out about business and work, and remember – you probably know far more than you think.**

Get some experience

Some work experience will help you back into working mode. To start with, this may be for a voluntary organisation to help you build up confidence. It could extend however to a work placement with an employer who is willing to take you on for a few days. This may help you define your career interests and reaffirm your commitment to a particular sector or job. Work experience won't turn you into a business tycoon in a week; but it will increase your confidence, give you an idea of what 'work' is like, give you a grasp of office terminology and antics, and an idea of what it's all about. At the very least, it will introduce you to working life.

Try local women's organisations

Organisations for professional women – like Soroptimists International – may have members who are willing to help you pick up some work experience. Contact the Club Secretary so that you can see whether a member could offer you something. Explain that you're seeking to go back to work and that you'd like a stint in the workplace to see how it has changed. If you can be specific about the sort of work you'd like to do, that will help.

You could try:

◆ informal lunch groups
◆ local branch of Women's Institute
◆ local women's pressure groups

◆ community service organisations, e.g. local Lions Club, Rotary, Soroptimists International
◆ organisation such as the Institute of Management and Institute of Directors
◆ school groups such as contacts in the PTA
◆ voluntary groups including the church.

The *Yellow Pages* or your local Citizens Advice Bureau should have the number of any local organisations which may be able to help you.

Visit your local Job Centre

Alternatively, you could go to your local Job Centre or Job Club to find out whether they could recommend a company you could approach who would help you or whether they are currently running a training programme which might be relevant to you.

Don't let people stamp on your dreams and goals just because you haven't done something in the past. Show those you talk to that you're willing to learn and start afresh with enthusiasm and drive.

Remember too that more and more women are starting their own business after raising a family of their own – and they are doing well at it. Common sense and stamina (of which you'll have plenty after years of raising children and/or running a home) are crucial.

Dealing with change

Change always involves a degree of risk. You know that, but going out to work, things will never be the same again. List all the times you've had to overcome fear in your life, from a small child to the adult you are now. How have you overcome those fears each time? What was it that made you so fearful? Going into the unknown, looking a fool, making a mistake or being a staggering success?

Fear is natural and can be overcome, as the section below shows. First, here's a comment from Lorri, who went back to teaching after eight years' break:

Case study: Lorri, returning to teaching _____

I arrived at the school in plenty of time on my first morning. My stomach was like a tight ball, I was gripping the steering wheel as if somebody was going to try to take it from me. I felt sick and shaky. 'I can't,' I kept thinking, 'I just can't'. I drove round and round the car park until suddenly, somehow, I had parked the car. I got out, walked into the school's main door. There was the familiar smell and noise of a school. The head teacher was coming towards me, smiling, 'Welcome, Lorri! I hope you'll be very happy here with us,' she greeted me, shaking me warmly by the hand. 'We're so glad you're here,' she continued, and suddenly, you know, so was I and I couldn't wait to get started. _____

Answering common fears

Sometimes, a person's job hunting or career plan don't come to anything because they are so afraid of failing that they deliberately *don't* do anything about them – if you don't do anything, you can't fail. But if you plan your move back into the job market carefully, you *won't* fail.

> **Plan carefully – more haste, less speed!**

Don't listen to your doubts – each of them can be answered positively.

'People like me are too old to learn anything'

A student aged 78 graduated with a degree last year. If she did it, you can. You only *think* you're too old. And there's the little matter of IT. Did you know that people over the age of 60 spend more time at home on their personal computers than young people do?

'Employers don't want people my age, anyway'

Not true. Employers are coming round to recognise that women returning to the workplace do have many skills and qualities to bring from their experiences of life so far.

'I failed at school – so I'm bound to fail now. What's the point?'

Adult education is very different from school. Lots of people who were absolute failures at school have excelled in adult education. Firstly, they are there because they want to be there; they are studying something they are naturally interested in and motivated to learn about. Secondly, there are now far more ways to study, one of which is bound to be suited to your favoured method of learning something.

'I don't know where to start!'

If you break your career planning down into small steps, as outlined in the next chapter, it all becomes more manageable and far more exciting, because you really are researching your ultimate goal.

'Why should I succeed?'

'I've failed in my main career – as a wife. How can I expect to succeed in anything else?' Michelle asked herself. Her husband had told her in no uncertain terms that she'd failed to live up to his ideal of the perfect wife. She believed her husband when he told her how useless she was, when he criticised her every move and never praised her for the things she did well.

Case study: Michelle's husband demolished her confidence _____
I know it sounds daft, but my four cats really kept me going, demanding their meals at normal times so that I did keep to some sort of routine. As the weeks wore on, I started to lose some of the numbness. People finally started to tell me how awful they thought Graham had been to me, and I began to realise it was *his* fault everything had gone wrong, not mine. And the cats helped; they had been such friends to me, I was terrified of losing them because I couldn't afford to keep them and they provided me with the kick I needed to get out of the house and get some money coming in. _____

Michelle finally recognised that *she* had not failed as a wife. Graham, had failed *her* as her husband. He had never supported her, had always put her down, nagged her, patronised her – these faults were his, not hers. She surrounded herself with supportive friends, who encouraged her to go back to work.

Try it now
- List everyone who may be affected by your return to work. Analyse how they might be affected and list the possible obstacles they may try to create. How would you overcome those?
- Identify any particular worries or fears you may have about returning to work; discuss them with somebody you trust who isn't going to brush them off by saying, 'Oh don't be silly.'
- Practise saying 'No' to people. It will come in handy later on and save you from overload.

Summary

Most barriers are overcome, but you need to tackle them as you go:
- Get the support of those closest to you by explaining why going back to work is important to you.
- Don't let a lack of confidence stop you trying things out – go for it!
- Spend time in the company of people who are positive about your going back to work and who will offer sensible suggestions and help. This is no time to put up with whiners.
- Don't waste energy feeling guilty. *You owe yourself this change.* Don't ignore your needs. You're important, too, you know.

| CHAPTER 4

Getting Ready for Action

I f you want to enjoy working, think carefully about the sort of job you want and how much time, energy and effort you wish to dedicate to it. After all, even if circumstances have forced you into the job market, you have a right to do something you're interested in, and you enjoy.

> **Life is too short to be unhappy in work.**

Career-planning skills and qualities

Every time you look for a new job, you'll need the information in this chapter.

Be honest with yourself and those you meet in your job hunting. Be determined – even if you've been rejected, keep trying. What have you said all those times to your daughter after she and her boyfriend have split up? 'Never mind, there'll be other fish in the sea.' The same is true of employers: one you had hopes for may have rejected you, but another will take you on. It's a matter of finding that one. Be open-minded about your options and learn as much as you can about yourself and the opportunities available to you.

Keep at it

Persistence and the ability to keep questioning everyone, from friends and family to personnel managers and Job Centre staff, will pay off. You may be told, 'No, we haven't got anyone recruiting for a secretary at the moment. Sorry, can't help you.' This isn't very helpful. *Push* your helper for more information. Could they recommend any employers who may at least be interested in your skills?

Sometimes people say, 'Oh, I rang so and so. They were useless – they couldn't tell me on the spot.'

Give people time to help you. Your questions may need thought and the person you're calling may be in the middle of a crucial project, or about to go into an important meeting. So give them a chance to come back to you.

Skills and qualities you'll need

Get advice and help from friends and family – they will be able to help you identify your strengths and weaknesses, skills and qualities. They will help you blow your own trumpet when you may feel too shy to do so.

You'll need enthusiasm, motivation and cheerful determination, and an ability to root out information. Most employers are pleased to help, especially if you appear to be serious about your career. Prior research shows you're not wasting an employer's time – for example, trips to the library to collect information and contact with professional bodies for up-to-date literature will prove that you are serious about your job hunt.

Job hunting also requires these skills:

◆ Communication skills: to ask questions and listen carefully to the answers; to write letters for information, or thanking people for their help; to talk things over with other people about your situation – and theirs.

◆ Research skills to find things out for yourself, such as using a library; using information technology (don't panic) and knowing how to find things out.

◆ Decision-making skills: the ability to make a decision, to stick with it and carry it through.

◆ The ability to plan and organise your goal of finding work – and to see it through. You need to know where you're going and what you want to achieve.

Using your network

The idea behind networking is that you use contacts you have – friends, past employers, organisations – to get information that will move your career planning forward. Networking does *not* necessarily involve asking people for a job, although of course you may find that job offers come your way as the word goes round that you're looking for work.

The recruiting process is a long and costly process for employers. Consequently, word of mouth is frequently used as a method to recruit. If you know someone who is working in the sort of organisation you'd like to work for, ask them to keep their ear to the ground for you. Personal recommendation is often very effective, especially if the person doing the recommending is highly thought of in the company.

Establishing your network

You probably have a vast network which you have used in the past to get all sorts of information; perhaps you have even contacted people you don't know for advice, because they've been recommended to you by a friend or someone you know professionally.

Example 1

Jean meets Debbie and realises she can provide useful information about secondary schools.

'Hello, Jean. How are you?'

'Oh, Debbie, I'm sorry – I can't stop. I'm so busy today. We're looking at schools for Diana – she's moving up into secondary in a couple of years and I'm trying to get home to make some phone calls before the staff go home. You know, for brochures, stuff like that.'

'I know, Jean – you need as much information as you can get these days, don't you?'

'Where does Jenny go, anyway?'

'She's gone to Gladstone's in Strawberry Avenue. We're very pleased with it. And she loves it – spending a lot of time doing outdoor sports, she's doing well in her languages, and they've got a trip to France next summer.'

'Oh, Debbie, Strawberry Avenue's not far from where we live – it would be one of the school's Diana could go to. Do you think I could pop round sometime to talk to you about it?'

'Yes, of course, Jean. You've got my number – I'll make sure

Jenny is at home. She can show you the sort of homework she's doing and tell you what she thinks.'

'Thanks, Debbie. I'm so glad I bumped into you.'

Jean has made an initial start using her network of friends to find out about schools for her daughter. Her next step is to actually meet with Debbie and Jenny to get more information.

Example 2

Clare meets her friend – and therefore contact – who works for a recruitment agency.

'Hello, Mary, how are you? I haven't seen you for a long time.'

'Oh, I'm fine thanks, Clare. Busy you know. I'm working in a recruitment agency in the High Street and business is booming. We're looking for a new secretary at the moment to help us with all the extra work.'

'Really? What sort of businesses are recruiting?'

'Oh, everyone – banks, building societies, financial advisers, you name it, they want people. What are you doing?'

'Well, actually I'm about to go back to work. I'd love to drop in and talk to you at some stage. Do you think that would be all right?'

'Yes of course. Bring your CV with you – here's my card. Just give us a call and set up a time, though, to see me – then I can make sure I have time to spend with you.'

'Thanks a lot, Mary. I'll do that!'

Clare has learnt that businesses are actively recruiting, she's made a contact who's willing to help her and all she needs to do now is to make sure her CV is up to date and follow up Mary's suggestion to get in touch.

Here you can see how two women have used their network to get information to help them make informed decisions about the future. Neither have been pushy to the extent of asking for a job or demanding help – guaranteed to put busy people's backs up.

Building your networking skills

Think of three past examples of networking you've done.
- Who did you approach for information?
- What other sources of information did you use?
- How effective were your sources?
- How confident did you feel asking questions?
- How much did you learn?

> **You already have a network of people you turn to for advice and information.**

There are some do's and don'ts to remember if you are going to network successfully:

Do
- think up questions to ask in advance of any meetings and write to thank anyone who has helped you for their time and advice;
- smile, be polite and enthusiastic;
- remember that your circumstances are different from the person you're talking to. Read between the lines;
- enjoy yourself!

Don't
- be aggressive and demand a job, or be pushy if you can't get the help you want;
- assume that everything you're told is up to date, especially if you're getting your information from friends: check with the professional body for the right answers because things do change quickly;
- be swayed or manipulated by others.

Talk to other women

Other women will tell you what it was like when they went back to work; what surprised them and what didn't. You can pick up useful ideas of how they coped, strategies that you might find yourself using in the future, for example with bosses who were younger and more aggressive than they were. Other women returnees will also be able to tell you what it was like to get to grips with information technology and describe what the workplace is like and how work differs from home. Women are natural networkers, able and willing to pull together and help each other out by sharing experiences and information. Make the most of it!

Draw up a job-hunting plan

A job-hunting plan will help you:

◆ save time, effort and energy
◆ find a job that you really want
◆ take action with more confidence and determination
◆ make the whole thing less daunting.

There are several parts to any job-hunting plan as the summary in Figure 2 shows. The amount of planning required, as shown in Figure 2, might seem daunting but remember that you make many decisions every day, some larger than others. Here are some examples:

Big decisions	Small decisions
Where are we going to move to?	What shall I wear today?
Where are we going to go on holiday this year?	What shall I cook for supper tonight?
Which school should Abby go to next term?	What shall I put in Joe's lunchbox today?

In each case, you have to weigh up a number of pieces of information and use them to decide what you're going to do. That is also the principle you'll apply to the process of finding a job.

> **Remember – you are already a skilled decision maker.**

Finding time to job hunt

Take a serious and professional approach to your career

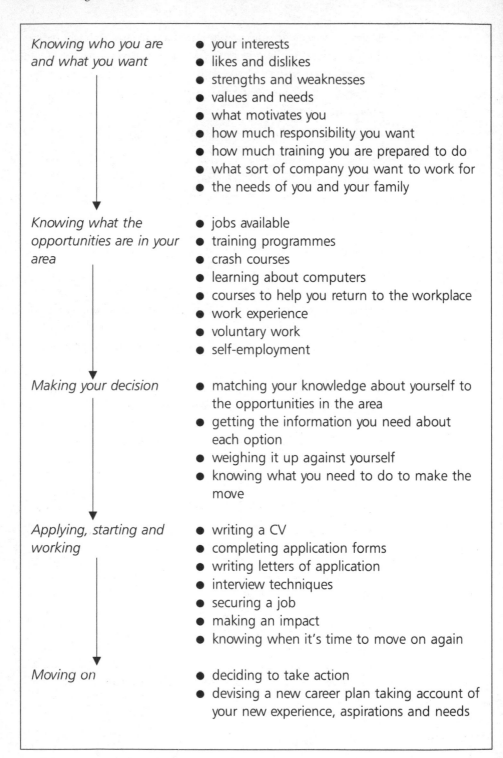

Knowing who you are and what you want	● your interests ● likes and dislikes ● strengths and weaknesses ● values and needs ● what motivates you ● how much responsibility you want ● how much training you are prepared to do ● what sort of company you want to work for ● the needs of you and your family
Knowing what the opportunities are in your area	● jobs available ● training programmes ● crash courses ● learning about computers ● courses to help you return to the workplace ● work experience ● voluntary work ● self-employment
Making your decision	● matching your knowledge about yourself to the opportunities in the area ● getting the information you need about each option ● weighing it up against yourself ● knowing what you need to do to make the move
Applying, starting and working	● writing a CV ● completing application forms ● writing letters of application ● interview techniques ● securing a job ● making an impact ● knowing when it's time to move on again
Moving on	● deciding to take action ● devising a new career plan taking account of your new experience, aspirations and needs

Fig. 2. A detailed job-hunting plan.

planning from the outset – you're far more likely to find the job you want. Finding a job takes anything from a couple of days to several months, depending on the local economy, your commitment to finding a job, how much training you need before you go out to work and – it has to be said – a bit of luck.

Put time aside to share your thoughts about your future with people you trust. These might include a careers adviser, family and friends and your partner. Spend time showing those who love you and who've relied on you so much over the years that they are still important to you. In particular, if you have a partner, make sure that you have time to talk and have fun, to do things as a couple.

Time to think

Put aside some time each day to think about your career planning.

Case study: Maggie, now a proofreader working from home _____
I thought about my day and the time when I'm at my most positive. I'm a morning person, so I put an hour aside every morning after my husband, Ron, left the house, to do my career planning. It was a good move, because I did it before starting all the mundane tasks which sometimes left me feeling that I was *just* a housewife. _____

People often procrastinate because they fear failure and so tell themselves – logically – 'Well, if I don't do anything, I won't fail.' So:

◆ Set yourself a given period of time to do something, e.g. by the end of the week you will have contacted your local colleges to find out what short courses they run which might be relevant to you;
◆ challenge your fears – what's the worst that could happen if things go wrong?
◆ set yourself daily targets, too, such as 'I'll make that phone call to the agency before the kids get home from school so that I can call when the house is quiet';
◆ go against the clock to get the task done;
◆ break down your action plan into stages.

Getting your resources together

Keep any thoughts in a careers file – so that you can refer back
to them, put in the 'Try it now' exercises at the end of each
chapter of this book, together with any articles and information
you find.

A word processor

Most employers prefer letters and CVs to be typed or produced
on a word processor, unless they specifically state otherwise. If
you don't have a typewriter or word processor at home, local
job centres, job clubs, education establishments' careers centres
and training schemes may be able to help. Try friends with
computers or local typists offering their services.

If there is a Job Club in your town, visit it – you should
find many facilities there, such as a photocopier to copy any
correspondence you send to employers, a telephone to arrange
interviews and a word processor. You'll meet other people who
are also returning to work or who have been unemployed.
There may be a small shop near you which offers a
photocopying and fax service. And keep a good supply of *first*
class stamps ready to use, too.

Your wardrobe and your image

Make sure you have an interview outfit available, clean and
pressed. A suit and blouse is a safe bet – especially if you're
interviewing for a position with customer services; in the media
things are more relaxed. Have a well-heeled, sensible pair of
shoes and a good hair cut. If somebody calls you in for an
interview with little warning, you've got an outfit ready. If
you're not sure what people wear for work at the place where
you're being interviewed, try to watch the staff arrive and leave
one day to sneak a preview of what the dress code is. Dress *up*
for the interview but tone *down* the jewellery, make-up and
perfume.

Financial resources

Once you have a job, you'll need to find out from the employer how the organisation intends paying you and you may need to set up a bank account in your own name. Talk with your partner about whether you want the money put into a joint account – perhaps his salary is already going in that direction – or whether you want an account of your own.

Don't forget – it costs money to work! Amongst other things, you'll need to pay for:

◆ transport to work and possibly car parking if you drive
◆ your work clothes unless a uniform is provided
◆ meals (there may be a subsidised canteen in some larger firms)
◆ coffee and tea in some organisations – others provide it free of charge
◆ socialising after work or in the lunch hour with your new colleagues
◆ tax and national insurance – get details from your local tax office
◆ care costs for children and/or dependant adults.

IT can help you plan your career

The Internet is an important job-hunting tool, not least because you can access plenty of information on education, employment and training opportunities, not just in your area, but also those which you can do from home. You can gain access to the Internet at your local college or library, Internet cafes or ask a friend if you can borrow her computer for an hour. The Internet is a mine of information including:

◆ *Jobs themselves.* Many recruitment firms, such as Reed and Office Angels, and web-sites such as www.fish4.co.uk advertise vacancies on the Internet, so you can get a lot of information without even making a phone call. They also offer lots of advice on job hunting and information on salaries in your area.
◆ *Information about specific companies.* You can also get a lot of information about companies from their web-sites on the computer. Well worth a read, if you can get access.
◆ *Educational institutions.* Most universities and many colleges are now present on the Internet. You can use sites such as Learn Direct and UCAS to find the best course for you.

♦ *Information on practical support, if you need it.* You can check out government departments, childcare advice.

♦ *Sites such as* www.ivillage.co.uk/workcareer with lots of advice and helpful information, for example, *16 ways to juggle your work and children*; www.womenback2work. co.uk with all sorts of tips on issues such as childcare, job-hunting and interview techniques; and www.femail.co.uk of the *Daily Mail* and *Mail on Sunday.*

Learn how to use the Internet

If you do not know how to use the Net, contact your local college or Learn Direct to find out what courses are available. Private training companies can also point you in the right direction. A basic computer class will teach you to know your way around the computer and handle a mouse. Classes will teach you how to search the Internet, how to handle and receive emails, create your own web page (useful if you want to run your own business) – and how you and business can make the most of it as a resource and marketing tool. You can learn all this on a computer without leaving home, but as a woman returner, you may have had enough of being at home and want to learn alongside new people.

Talk to an adviser at your local college

They will talk to you about the experience you've had with computers and recommend the best class for you. This may be held during the day or one evening a week.

Don't despair

If you still feel more comfortable talking to a human being and flicking through the pages of a book, this next section will help you find people who can help too.

They should have up-to-date and well stocked libraries for you to refer to.

Identifying other sources of help

> People will help and advise you, every step of the way –
> even those you don't know!

The range (and quality) of provision in terms of training
programmes, opportunities and careers advice will vary
throughout the country. Make contact with the organisations
listed below to find out what they can do for you as a woman
returning to work – they may run programmes specifically
designed for you.

Careers services

The old local education authority services have been privatised
and are now careers service companies. Their main goal is to
meet the needs of young people, but many help adults who
wish to go back to education, training or employment. Some
may charge. Check the *Yellow Pages* for their telephone
number and address; your local library may have details of the
company nearest you and the sorts of services they offer.

Careers service companies may offer you the chance to do a
computer programme which will assess your strengths, interests,
likes and dislikes, together with your current qualifications and
desire to train or study further, and come up with a number of
careers which might suit you.

Learning and Skills Council

Training and Enterprise Councils were replaced by Learning
and Skills Councils, which are now responsible for ensuring
that the needs of local communities – organisations and
individuals – are met. It's their job to ensure that learning
opportunities meet local skills' needs and they work with
businesses to forecast their requirements and make sure that
they are met. They should therefore have information on local
labour market trends, training programmes and short courses
for those seeking to run their own business.

Your local library

Many libraries have corners dedicated to careers, together with computers to help you find out more information about opportunities available.

Like the local careers service companies, the library should have lots of up-to-date information about careers, education and training opportunities. Pay them a visit to find out what they have to offer.

The Job Centre

The Job Centre should know which employers in town like to recruit the mature person, as opposed to the youngster. Ask them to point you in the right direction. They will also have a listing of job vacancies in the local area, and, usefully, they will have details of local training programmes which might be relevant to you, with details of any benefits you're entitled to.

Education providers

There are a great many of these and Chapter 9 gives further details.

The National Institute of Adult Continuing Education (NIACE) (see Useful Addresses) is the national organisation for all adult learning. One of its roles is to provide an information and advice service for organisations and individuals and to co-ordinate Adult Learners' Week, which is a nationwide event designed to promote adult education and training opportunities. Local educational providers will inevitably get involved and put on exhibitions or conventions of what's on offer locally.

Learning Direct is a helpline which offers free information and advice on learning opportunities and careers for adults. All the advisers are experienced adult guidance counsellors. See Useful Addresses.

Private industry

Human resources departments are involved in recruiting, training and developing staff to meet the needs of the organisation and its future. Personnel departments are more likely to deal with straight recruitment. Training departments organise training programmes for staff designed to meet the needs of an organisation. Human resource departments and personnel departments may be able to send you any careers information produced by their company.

Recruitment companies

Recruitment companies should not charge you for registering with them. They help companies recruit a range of staff; Chapter 12 describes the process you would go through. Look for a company that is a member of the professional organisation, REC (Recruitment and Employment Confederation).

Careers consultants

You may see these advertised in national and local newspapers or women's magazines. Be prepared to pay for them. Make sure you know what you'll get for your money and find out what qualifications the advisers have before you commit yourself.

> Take time to build a picture of local sources of help.

The press

The local paper provides local vacancy information in the recruitment pages, and details of college courses. Many run careers supplements prior to the start of the academic year. Local press will also give you clues as to which companies are expanding and which are 'downsizing', or shedding staff, and the names of recruitment companies and those involved in personnel whom you might approach for advice or to enquire about details.

National papers frequently offer advice from personnel managers and recruitment personnel about all sorts of issues concerning job hunting. Articles may be of a general nature, such as what to wear for an interview, or how to write a CV; or

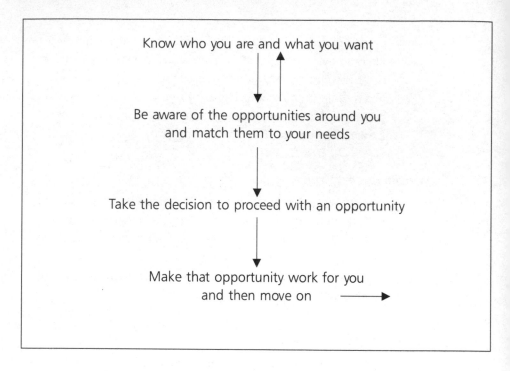

Fig. 3. A career plan.

they may be more specialised, covering areas such as 'Careers with animals' or 'Careers for the listener'. Papers have their own web-sites: some, such as the *Daily Mail* and *Mail on Sunday*, have pages aimed at women, with www.femail.co.uk.

The press may report on new developments in career areas, such as new ways to train for something which has previously had only one route in. It may also explain the plethora of new qualifications which have appeared in recent years.

Other sources of help:

◆ Your own network of friends and family, some of whom may know of someone who's looking to recruit.
◆ Professional bodies which set and maintain the standards of particular industries; you can find their addresses in the book *Occupations* which will be in your local library.

Try it now	◆ List everyone you know in your network who is at work or studying in adult education; note their phone numbers and the name of the company they work for. Put your list in your careers file for use when you're doing your research.
	◆ Find out what help is available in your area from those you don't know, as outlined in the above section.
	◆ Think out a plan for your career, along the lines of Figure 3, using the exercises in this book to help you.

Summary

Career planning requires thought and dedication if you are to find the right opportunity for you.

+ Thorough research will pay dividends.
+ Don't expect to get a job straightaway – it will take time to find the job you really want.
+ Use your network – ask people plenty of questions about how they did it, what advice they would have and whether they know of people who can help you.

CHAPTER 5

Analysing Your Skills

I f you take the time to look at your own skills, you will probably find that you can offer employers many of the skills they need particularly today. Flexibility, adaptability, caring, teamwork, coping with change, networking and cooperating with others, are all strong skills women have.

Assessing yourself is a must

Self-assessment is a vital part of career planning. Many people feel shy about it, especially if they are not used to thinking about their strengths, interests, values and needs.

Case study: Angela, now a Financial Adviser ⎯⎯⎯⎯⎯⎯⎯⎯⎯

The hardest bit for me was sitting down after all these years after looking after a family and trying to concentrate on *my* needs, and what *I* wanted. It was terribly difficult at first to focus and it certainly took a bit of practice; but thinking about my skills, projects and my interests helped me think about what I'm good at and enjoy doing. ⎯⎯⎯⎯⎯⎯⎯⎯⎯

Learn to assess yourself with confidence!

As a result of analysing your skills you will

1 have a better idea of what you want out of a job;

2 gain self-confidence;

3 be able to deal with possible attempts by family and friends to put you off going out to work – easier when you have a clear goal to aim for;

4 know exactly what information you need;

5 develop the skills you want to use at work;

6 know where your weaknesses are and identify gaps in your knowledge and skills so that you can do something about them;

7 be able to talk about your achievements and abilities in interview and sell yourself to an employer;

8 go into any selection situation with a real sense of pride and achievement;

9 learn something about yourself that you never knew before;

10 be able to tell a company what you can do for them.

In this and the next three chapters there will be lots of self-assessment exercises for you to do. The only right answers are honest ones. When you have completed each exercise, share your answers with someone you trust who will be honest with you. Do they agree with your answers? If not, why not? What examples can they come up with of skills you've demonstrated recently?

Defining 'work'

When people think of the term 'work', they often think in terms of employment, i.e. a job.

Work = a job

or, better still:

Work = a paid job

There's more to the word 'work' than that, however.

Work = effort

'Work' covers paid employment in a job, but it also means doing a task or duty which involves a physical or mental effort. Playing tennis requires physical effort and so it's work. Doing patchwork is work, so is driving a car, cooking, cleaning, being a member of a committee – they all require physical and mental work and motivation. The teacher in front of a biology class, the leisurely swimmer in the pool, the Brownie studying for a badge and the lady selling raffle tickets to raise money for charity are all working in one way or another, and each is using a different combination of skills and abilities.

At work, you'll need a range of skills – and you'll find that you have many of these already:

◆ *basic skills* – literacy, numeracy, plus information technology (i.e. the ability to read, write and do sums, and to use a computer)

◆ *transferable skills* – such as communicating, team work, managing yourself; these are often known as 'soft skills'

◆ *job-specific skills* – those skills which you need to do the particular job you do, for example, to arrange flowers if you are a florist

◆ *leadership skills* – taking charge, taking risks, strategic management, vision, the ability to lead and motivate people, to plan and implement. You'll need these if you want to run your own business and lead others at the helm of a company, or in a team.

Throughout life, you will have developed a broad range of skills and abilities which can be applied to the workplace.

In Chapter 1, you listed all the activities you do. Revise your list to make sure that it covers the following, both past and present:

◆ leisure activities

◆ your achievements – no matter how small you think they are

◆ any projects you've worked on, e.g. your daughter's wedding, moving house

◆ any courses

◆ voluntary work

◆ past work experience

◆ memberships of organisations or clubs

◆ positions you hold on a committee, e.g. Women's Institute, PTA, church group etc.

They have all enabled you to develop many skills and abilities. Use your list as you work through the next few chapters to analyse the skills and qualities you have.

Looking at basic skills

Can you read and write? Have you got basic mathematical

skills? These things are essential if you are to apply for a job successfully. *All* employers need staff with basic skills – even though most computers have a spellcheck facility, that check will offer you a number of options and you'll still need to know which is the right word.

Getting help

If your basic skills are lacking, improve them at your local college. You'll probably be given one-to-one tuition with a patient tutor who really does want to help you. There are also courses which recognise that some of us have basic skills which are rusty or which we never felt confident using – hence you might find your local college offering courses called 'Mathematics for the Terrified' or 'Basic Mathematics'. Many offer support and help in areas such as writing essays and/or reports, spelling, grammar and maths – decimals, percentages and fractions for example. If you have particular learning difficulties, you will have help with these too.

The Basic Skills Agency is a national development agency for literacy, numeracy and related basic skills in England and Wales. It seeks to help people overcome any difficulties they have with these skills. If you want to improve your basic skills, you can call the Learn Direct helpline and they will help you find a course.

Boosting your IT skills

Virtually every job has been affected by IT so employers also want people with basic computer abilities. You don't have to be a computer whiz; most employers will be happy if you know your way around the keyboard, aren't afraid of the computer in front of you and have an idea of how to look after it, e.g. not to spill coffee over it. Chapter 10 gives more information on how you can boost your IT skills.

You may already use IT at home, perhaps to order your supplies from a supermarket, to do research, or to send emails to friends and relatives. List everything you use your computer for. It demonstrates a willingness to use IT and shows that you are competent in using it for certain functions. Keep examples of your work – letters, emails and responses, use of the Internet. You may be able to use this to gain a National Vocational Qualification in IT (see Chapter 9).

Excelling at communication

Communication skills are vital in the workplace.

> **Women excel at communicating with a very wide range of people.**

Checklist all those people you've communicated with over the last two weeks.

- Who were they?
- How did you communicate?
- What sort of language and tone did you adopt?
- How many were on a business basis, e.g. the gas, or phone company?
- Could you have handled the situation more effectively?
- How do you think the other person felt after the communication between you?

Think of times when you have presented a case to somebody, done some public speaking, complained about a service or product, given constructive criticism, negotiated (perhaps with your children?), dealt with conflict, handled a very sensitive situation, participated in a meeting of any sort. Being assertive is an important skill, too, which involves communicating in a clear, direct and open manner while understanding the other person's viewpoint.

Communicating with people also involves asking them to do something for you on occasion and delegating work. These are all invaluable communication skills which you will use daily at work, handling customers or colleagues. Using the telephone is also an important skill which involves answering the call promptly, speaking clearly and ensuring that the other person understands what the call is about and that a conclusion is reached.

Listening is a key skill, too. In many jobs you need to have the ability to listen to what people *are not* telling you, as well as what they *are* saying. And the way we greet people always makes an impression: a smile, a warm welcome, plenty of eye contact and a positive approach will make a great difference to a customer's impression of a company.

Showing you can handle routine

Routine is important – it's the thing that keeps the business or home going from day to day. *Every* job has routine tasks, however high-powered it is. Some people enjoy routine, while others try hard to avoid it.

Your routine activities might include:

◆ shopping
◆ cleaning
◆ washing and ironing
◆ cooking, deciding on menus
◆ gardening
◆ caring for children, pets and elderly relatives
◆ dealing with bills, budgeting
◆ maintaining the home.

> **Routine is important in any business. You already handle routine tasks well.**

Even routine work demands skills and qualities

Housework demands manual dexterity – strong and supple hands. You use organisational skills to manage your time, working out what needs to be done first and dealing with interruptions as they occur. You constantly motivate yourself – things won't get done if you slump in front of the television – and you persuade and motivate others (e.g. your partner to mow the lawn). You work without supervision and just get on with things. All these skills and qualities will be useful at work.

Managing yourself

At work today employers need people who can manage themselves and work both on their own and in a team. This section looks at some of the qualities you need to be able to manage yourself.

Women are brilliant jugglers. We can handle several things at the same time, paying attention to someone on the phone, while a toddler pulls at our skirt or delves into something he shouldn't, and cooking dinner. You need to juggle at work, too. You might have one customer on the phone, your boss wants to see you, you know you have to send someone an email and somebody else a fax. When was the last time you had to handle several things at once, or several projects at once? How did you cope?

Making good use of time

How good are you at organising yourself and your time? Can you easily spot your priorities during the day, the week, the month and the year? Do you plan well ahead or leave everything until the last minute? Can you take a project, divide it into small chunks of work, do that work in the right and logical order, so that it gets finished on time? If you're asked to help organise a coffee morning for charity, can you safely be relied upon to sort out your bit, whether it be selling raffle tickets, asking people to donate prizes for the raffle or persuading people to make cakes to sell? Do you do this sort of thing in good time, or at the last minute?

How well do you cope with stress?

Some people get more stressed than others. Certain situations worry some people more than others. Which difficult situations do you find easier to deal with, and which harder?

Think about how well you work under pressure. Do you grit your teeth and get on with it, or let everything fall apart and give up trying to control a situation?

Delivering what you promise

Being nice to customers means nothing if you don't do what you said you would for them. Think of a time when one company met a deadline over something that was important to you and another time when a company didn't.

1   How did you feel about the company that did deliver?

2 And how did you feel about the one that didn't make it?

3 Which would you use again in the future?

Do you always deliver what you say you will? How often? 100 per cent of the time? 80 per cent? 20 per cent? or not at all?

Consider what sort of results are important to you. What do you want to achieve? This is important because many roles will involve seeking to reach numerical targets, such as a set number of sales in a store, a profit margin or a ranking in the industry. Others will involve a more humanitarian result, such as moving an individual forward in an aspect of their life (counselling) or bringing out the best in somebody (teacher). Think about what you want to achieve on the job.

Working in a team

Some people are natural team players. They participate in team sports, play a part on committees, look forward to working with other people and to doing their bit. They have their own principles and views, but are prepared to compromise when necessary in favour of the bigger picture. If they are suddenly asked to join a team to get something done – for example, to take part in organising a jumble sale to raise money quickly to send to earthquake victims on the other wide of the world – they are happy to jump in at once and do what they can, working alongside people they don't necessarily know.

Other people are distinctly uncomfortable doing things in a group and prefer to do things on their own. Visiting the cinema or theatre, reading, swimming, cycling or cooking are all activities that are done alone; they do not need more than one person to be involved.

Obviously, many of us combine team and solo activities: Margaret loves a game of tennis with her three friends, but she also loves knitting. She has a wide span of interests, which show an employer that she's a team player, but also someone who can do things on her own.

◆ How many of your activities involve working with a group of people, either for leisure, interest or work?

◆ How much do you enjoy working with others in a team to

achieve a goal? Can you show that you have done this in the past? What was your contribution?

◆ Describe something you have done in a team recently. What part did you play? What about the others in the team? What did they do?

If you do not enjoy working with other people, look for a job which does not require much contact with them. An example? In one episode of Victoria Wood's sitcom *Dinner Ladies*, the temporary catering manager suddenly realises that she doesn't like working with people – and so she heads off to apply for a job in a lighthouse!

Are you a leader?

Team activities can give you good insight into the sort of role you veer to – whether you like to be the leader of the pack, or prefer to be in a supporting role in environments you don't know. When you are working in a team of people, what sort of role do you like to play? Do you automatically find yourself seeking to take charge and lead a project, pulling people together and ensuring that everything is running smoothly? Some people are quite happy to be in a supporting role, whereby others take the major decisions, such as where an organisation is going and how they are going to get there. Think about how much of a leader you are – if you like running the show, why not think about running your own business.

Take a piece of paper and rate yourself for each of the skills we have just discussed under the headings Very good/Good/Not bad/Awful:

◆ juggling
◆ planning ahead
◆ organising
◆ prioritising
◆ working in a team
◆ working on your own
◆ working under pressure.

In each case, think of two specific examples of times you've had to use these skills, both in and out of the house, and list them.

Then file your sheet in your career file for later reference.

Building your skills base

Many of the skills you use at home can be transferred across to the workplace:

Skill used at work	Examples of how you use them at home
Organising	dinner party, jumble sale
Planning	specific event in the future, your week in advance
Juggling	doing several things at once in a hurry
Prioritising	deciding what needs to be done first
Long-term budgeting	for something specific, e.g. a new washing machine
Short-term budgeting	for routine needs, e.g. the shopping
Researching information	schools for children, holidays
Negotiating	with the children about bed time
Persuading	people to do things they don't want to do
Leading	a group, the family
Creating	ideas for children to do on a rainy summer day
Recruiting	plumber, electrician, cleaner
Selling things	raffle tickets, flag day, Oxfam shop
Motivating others	the kids to tidy their rooms
Stamina	keeping going from dawn to midnight

These are all skills which are used in running a home, bringing up children, doing voluntary work, taking part in leisure activities and so on. As you analyse your past for evidence of such skills, you are demonstrating that you have abilities in the following areas which are necessary in the world of work:

- managing yourself
- showing you can deliver
- communication skills
- carrying out routine work
- working in a team
- basic skills.

Still not convinced? Here's an example:

Example: Christmas

You use many skills and qualities at Christmas or at any other festive time, including:

- *negotiating* with relatives – where will Christmas day be spent and who is to be there?
- *planning* Christmas itself – food, presents, clothes, fitting routine work in;
- *time management* to ensure that everything is ready when it should be;
- *stress management* so that you can cope with it all;
- *budgeting* to decide how much money you want to spend;
- *delegating* to others to help you out, for example your partner to buy the tree;
- *advising* everyone on presents to buy;
- *manual dexterity* in writing cards and wrapping presents;
- *resourcefulness* in ensuring your money goes further;
- *keeping up routine work* – cleaning, shopping, ironing, looking after pets;
- *entertaining* friends, relatives and neighbours more than usual, especially dealing with the 'we were just passing and thought we'd pop in' brigade;
- *coping* with kids home for the holidays and keeping them occupied;
- *stamina*.

> All these skills are transferable. They can be used in a variety of jobs.

Identifying job-specific skills you want to use

Every job has specific skills it alone needs, which run parallel to the transferable ones everybody requires at work. The job-specific skills demanded by a public relations officer and a dentist are totally different. You must now consider which job-specific skills you'd like to use 'on the job', and those which you are good at or want to learn how to use. If you are involved in voluntary work and sitting on committees, it may well be easier to identify skills you naturally veer towards – you have offered to do these tasks for an organisation because you know you'll do them well.

From the following list of skills, note down which ones you:

1   use regularly

2   are good at using

3   enjoy using

4   would like to use at work

5   have not had the chance to use before, but would like to try.

This will help you determine what you want to do all day.

absorbing details	comparing	editing
achieving	conducting	empathising
acting	conserving	establishing something
adapting	controlling	examining
administering	coordinating	explaining
arranging	coping in emergencies	financing
assembling	counselling	fund-raising
assessing	creating	generating business
advising	cultivating	giving
advocating	debating	greeting
analysing	decision-making	growing
answering questions	delivering	guiding
arguing	demolishing	handling
assimilating	demonstrating	identifying opportunities
book-keeping	designing	implementing
budgeting	developing people/ideas	initiating
building	dispensing	inspecting
caring for others	displaying	intervening
checking facts/figures	drafting	interviewing
classifying	drawing	investigating
coaching others	driving	investing

keeping records
leading
learning
listening
lobbying
managing
marketing
massaging
mediating
mending
monitoring
motivating others
navigating
negotiating
networking
organising
persuading
presenting
prioritising
probing
processing

promoting
proving
protecting
public speaking
publishing
purchasing
questioning
reading
recalling
recording
recruiting
registering
regulating
relaying information
renewing
repairing
reporting
researching
reviewing
seeking advice
selling

serving others
showing
solving problems
supervising
supporting
talking
taking minutes
teaching
telephoning
thinking rapidly
touching
tracing
training
transferring
transporting
travelling
tutoring
understanding
underwriting
welcoming
writing

Which of these skills would the following people particularly
need to do their jobs:

◆ teacher
◆ sales assistant
◆ nurse
◆ journalist.

Some jobs use one skill more than others; for example, a nurse
might teach a patient how to give himself an injection, whereas
a teacher teaches a class much of the time.

Most jobs involve several skills with an emphasis on one or
two very specific ones. A counsellor spends most of her time
counselling people – but she will also keep her records up to
date, market her own service to professionals and liaise with
other people in the medical profession about her patients. The
emphasis for her, however, will be on the counselling.

Looking at your list of the skills you enjoy using and those
you wish to use at work, look for jobs or career sectors which
want those skills.

> Be able to demonstrate how you've used your skills by giving particular examples.

Try it now

♦ Think of examples for every skill you have to show an employer that, yes, you can use that skill.

♦ Refer to the local papers to study the vacancies listed there. What skills do these require. Do you have them? Would you want to use them?

♦ Write down those skills you want to use most of all in a job – and those you'd rather not use at all! The ones you want to use are the ones to concentrate on.

Summary

Be proud of all you've achieved in and out of the home, remembering that:

♦ time taken to analyse your routine work and projects in and out of the home will enable you to identify skills you use regularly and enjoy using;

♦ the more informed you are about what you are good at and enjoy doing, the more you are likely to end up doing it – and enjoying it!

*You'll get more
out of life if you
know what's
important to
you*

CHAPTER 6

The Sort of Person You Are

I n today's job market you must be able to talk about your
achievements, what you do well and what you find difficult.
Self-knowledge and effective self-marketing are key tools in job
hunting.

Blow your own trumpet!

Below are a list of qualities. Note down those which describe
you. Which ones would you like to use 'on the job'?

absent-minded	a 'doer'	passionate
achiever	emotional	passive
accurate first time	efficient	patient
ambitious	energetic	practical
artistic	extrovert	private
assertive	flexible	pro-active
athletic	fast worker	punctual
calm	hard worker	relaxed
caring	healthy	reliable
charming	hospitable	reserved
cheerful	imaginative	respects privacy
compassionate	inquisitive	results-oriented
competitive	introvert	sense of humour
confident	kind	sensible
considerate	literate	sensitive
constructive	lively	shy
daring	loyal	sociable
decisive	methodical	a 'thinker'
dependable	moody	thorough
determined	nervous	tolerant
devoted	open-minded	untidy
direct	optimistic	welcoming

What do friends and family think?

Show your ranking to your partner, other family members or friends. Ask them whether they agree with your ranking and to suggest examples of things you've done with them that show your particular qualities. Find out too what they think your weaknesses are – and see whether you disagree with them! Don't be defensive – listen to what they have to say.

This information is useful because:

1   You'll know yourself better, and therefore know what you want in a future job.

2   You will be able to give a better picture of yourself using these adjectives throughout your application.

3   You may be asked in an interview what your strengths and weaknesses are. Having had examples of these will help you give full answers.

> **Knowing what makes you tick will help you decide what sort of job you want. Think about the sectors which need the qualities you have.**

Knowing your values and needs

Exercise 1

On a separate sheet of paper, copy and complete the questionnaire shown in Figure 4, and file it in your career folder for future reference. It will highlight what is important to you in a job and a company.

Exercise 2

On page 73, using a separate sheet of paper which you can file in your career folder, write down against each number the aspect mentioned which most appeals to you. This will give you a more detailed profile of the sort of job or company you might prefer:

Aspects of a job that are important to me	Essential	Fairly important	Doesn't matter	Not at all important
To enjoy it and have fun				
The salary: I need to earn £____ a month				
Being responsible for other members of staff, a team				
An employer who is sympathetic to families				
My colleagues				
Working conditions				
Journey time to work				
Opportunity to meet people				
Customer contact				
Chance to help others				
Hours				
Holiday entitlement				
Good training				
Lots of scope for career progression				
Flexible conditions				
A challenge				
The type of person I would serve				
No physical risk-taking				
Doesn't involve heights/heat/dust/dirt/cold				
Feeling valued by colleagues, bosses and customers				
Sense of belonging				

Fig. 4. A questionnaire to show which aspects of a job are important.

1 indoors/outdoors/mixture

2 local firm/national firm/international firm

3 large-sized firm/medium-sized firm/small-sized firm

4 lots of deadlines daily/very few deadlines at all

5 work for one firm/work for several/work for self

6 desk bound/car bound/moving about

7 travel around UK on the job/travel abroad on the job/no travelling on the job

8 performance related pay/salary or wage and commission/salary or wage

9 work from home all the time/work out of the house/part home-based

10 high profile position in organisation/just one of the team/work on own

11 very bureaucratic company/some bureaucracy in the company/no bureaucracy at all

12 lots of attention to detail/some attention to detail/no detail at all

13 lots of routine work/some routine/minimum amount of routine

14 lots of autonomy – can handle it on own/some autonomy in job/no autonomy at all – prefer to be told what to do

15 flexible working day/never knowing what is going to happen next day/knowing exactly what will happen

These exercises will show you what's important to you. Try to think why what you have chosen as essential is so important in each case.

> **Knowing what you want from a job helps to determine your options.**

Examples

- ◆ Liz knew she didn't want to spend more than 30 minutes getting to work every day – so she concentrated on searching for a job locally in a large town a bus ride away.
- ◆ Erica wanted to work for an international company and she didn't mind travelling an hour a day to get it – as a result she had three cities where she could look for work.
- ◆ Anita wanted to work very close to home so that she could pop back to let her dog out in the lunch hour – so she confined her search to the local shops.
- ◆ Annette wanted a job that brought her into lots of contact with the elderly – so she looked at all the organisations in her area which dealt with them.

All these people had things which were important to them. Every criteria they placed on the job they wanted meant that their choice of job was reduced, especially in Anita's case. Recognise your limits: if something is important to you, accept it.

> **The best route to get what you want may be to run your own business.**

Running your own business

Today, around three million people run their own business. Many people start their own business because they need the flexibility and feel that working for another organisation doesn't meet that need.

Advantages of working for yourself include:
- ◆ it may be easier to balance family life and work
- ◆ more choice in your working hours
- ◆ it's very satisfying to have your own business (when things are going well)
- ◆ you can work from home.

Disadvantages include:
- ◆ the hours can be very long and the holidays very few
- ◆ it can be very lonely
- ◆ the business could fail

◆ it may be difficult to 'leave the office'.

It's important to talk through this option with those you live with.

Try this test to see if you've got what it takes to run your own business. Are you:

entrepreneurial	energetic
determined	able to work on your own
focused	willing to forgo holidays at first
a risk taker	full of stamina
a clear thinker	competitive
resilient	organised
tough	highly motivated
creative	good at advertising yourself
willing to work hard	

Many women choose to run their own business

Talk to women in your area who run their own business to find out what the picture looks like, warts and all. You need to know that it's definitely for you before taking the plunge. You could set up as a sole trader, self-employed, a temp, a partnership with a friend or as a limited company.

Your local college may run a short course on running your own business. This may cover writing a business plan, raising the money, ensuring cashflow, how to do your own marketing and PR, as well as the accounting, tax and national insurance side. Check out the Federation of Small Businesses' web-site and your local Business Link (see Useful Address or visit the web-site) for lots of helpful advice and information. There's a New Deal scheme for those seeking to run their own business, helping you to decide whether it's right for you. The scheme can help in producing a business plan, and offer advice through the first six months while you get things off the ground. Contact your local bank and its competitors to see how they can help and advise people seeking to start their own business. Many produce helpful booklets designed at least to get you thinking; and many have small business advisers to help you get off the ground and expand.

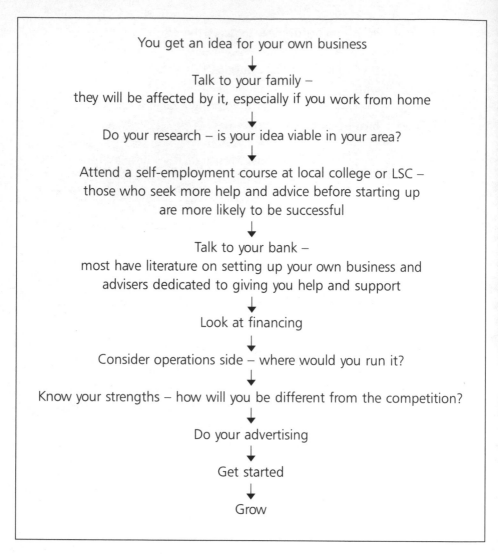

You get an idea for your own business

↓

Talk to your family –
they will be affected by it, especially if you work from home

↓

Do your research – is your idea viable in your area?

↓

Attend a self-employment course at local college or LSC –
those who seek more help and advice before starting up
are more likely to be successful

↓

Talk to your bank –
most have literature on setting up your own business and
advisers dedicated to giving you help and support

↓

Look at financing

↓

Consider operations side – where would you run it?

↓

Know your strengths – how will you be different from the competition?

↓

Do your advertising

↓

Get started

↓

Grow

Fig. 5. Planning your own business.

Figure 5 shows the steps you will have to work through in some detail in planning to run your own business.

Think about how you want to run your own business

You could buy your own franchise, which means that you usually have the backing and experience of the franchisor who will help you investigate the market in your area, offer you training and a number of resources; and who usually has a proven track record. You can buy a job franchise, in which you do all the actual work, e.g. delivering pet food. Or you can buy a management franchise, in which you recruit people to do the work for you and manage them and the business yourself. The amount of money you need to buy a franchise varies considerably, ranging from around £5,000 to £75,000 or more.

Any newsagent will sell a copy of magazines such as *Business Franchise*, which outlines many of the franchises available to the public. Most franchises have a proven track record and training programmes to help you get started. The British Franchise Association holds exhibitions during the year in various parts of the country – contact them for more information (see Useful Addresses). Many banks will have literature for those considering becoming a franchisee.

Looking at other alternatives

Many people work for companies such as Tupperware or Dorling Kindersley, which involves displaying the goods at small evening events of eight to 12 people, taking orders, ordering the goods required from the company and then delivering them when they arrive. You usually have somebody who is already working in an area close to you who supports you and most companies offer training programmes and conferences. This is a job you can do from home but it frequently involves evening and weekend work. However, it is up to you what you make of it – it can be full or part time, the choice is yours. Look out for such opportunities in the press.

Going freelance

If you have a specific skill or are an expert in an area of knowledge, you could put a price on your services and offer yourself as a freelance to firms. You would need to build up a network of prospective business contacts and you have no guarantee of regular work or income; but you can be independent, work from home and enjoy a greater variety of work. See Further Reading for more information.

Financial help available

This comes in all sorts of guises, from the Rural Development

Commission, set up to help people in rural areas establish and run their own businesses, to the local schemes run by your local LSC. See what information your LSC and local library has.

If your own bank is not supportive of your plans to run your own business, talk to another one. They may be quite happy to help you start up.

Working for an employer from home

Perhaps a family member is seriously ill or going through a rough patch, making it difficult to you to leave home. IT developments mean increasing numbers of people are able to work from home via a computer link to the office (usually set up and paid for by the company) or work from home as telemarketers. There are also a number of short courses you can do which give you the skills and knowledge it takes to work from home in an area such as proofreading and creative writing. If you work for a company at home, it is a good idea to visit the office regularly to keep in touch and abreast of training opportunities. You may be able to set your own hours in this line of work. For more information, contact the Telecottage Association whose addresses is listed in Useful Addresses.

Describing yourself

Using the information you have acquired so far about yourself, write a short up-to-date paragraph – a personal summary. Concentrate on:

◆ your career aspirations, areas of interest for work and how much research you've done;
◆ the skills you have and the qualities you can offer;
◆ what has motivated you to return to work;
◆ the sort of work you are looking for and the sort of company you want to work for.

This will help you focus the self-knowledge you have acquired so far and start to give you an idea of what you want to look for in a job.

Try it now
- Start relating your particular qualities to careers and roles.
- Check the local paper. Identify those posts which are calling for qualities such as yours.
- Look at five posts advertised in the local press. What skills and qualities do they call for? Do you have these? What training is required? Would that line of work interest you as a career?

Summary

Your best qualities are the ones which are most likely to make you happy at work if you can use them – because you will be more likely to excel at what you are doing.

1 Get as rounded a view as you can from friends, family and others who know you – even in just a few short words.

2 Keep adding to your thoughts – even when you start work.

3 Ask those helping you to give you examples of times you've displayed particular qualities – it will make them think harder, they are less likely to say something just for the sake of it and your confidence will increase!

CHAPTER 7

What Work Do You Want to Do?

Y ou've identified skills that you enjoy using and qualities which you would like to use at work. Now is the time to think about the career sector which interests you; and indeed whether you want a job where you can just arrive, do it and leave; or whether you want a fully-fledged career which might impinge on your life outside work occasionally.

Identifying areas that interest you

It is important to look for evidence of interest, so that you know you're not just kidding yourself. Many of our interests come naturally to us out of curiosity or trying new things out.

Ask yourself these questions and list the answers:

1   What do you really care about?

2   What would you do anything for? Or go the extra mile for?

3   Given half the chance, what would you talk about endlessly?

4   What do you love reading about?

5   What are the times you have enjoyed most in your life?

6   What were your favourite subjects at school? The ones you did best at?

7   What are your interests and hobbies now? Creative? Physical?

8   What voluntary work do you participate in? What appeals to you about it?

9   Is there anything you've always secretly wanted to do? A dream job?

Think about whether your interests involve your being with people, or on your own; whether you are with a large group of people or a small one. What activities do they involve exactly? Are they done outside or indoors?

Anything on your list may give you clues about the sort of job you're looking for, since the choices are your own. Look also to past jobs and roles you've had for clues of what has held your interest over the years.

Now think broadly and ask yourself:

1 What organisations exist to support those interests, issues and concerns? Put down every one you can think of against each of your interests, even if it does not concentrate exclusively on your interest. Figure 6 is an example of this sort of exercise.

2 What do they do?

3 What support networks do they have?

4 Could they use your skills, interest and knowledge?

5 Could you set up your own business around them?

Look in *Yellow Pages* and surf the Internet for companies in your area that connect with your interests and add them to your list. You may know of people who work for them already, or perhaps are a past customer. By looking at your interests and listing companies which deal with them, you have just identified a large number of employers whom you might approach to see if they could use your skills and abilities!

Case study: Faith, working in a sports complex _____

I've always been interested in sports and leisure and thought it would be fun to work in an environment where people were coming in because they wanted to. When my husband suddenly left me, and I needed a job, a friend asked me if I'd like to work in a new health centre as a receptionist. I *adore* it – I love meeting the people and working in a place which naturally interests me. I'm going to study for a health promotion qualification, next. _____

> It's much easier to keep learning and provide an excellent service if you're naturally interested in something.

My interests	Organisations that match those interests
Cats	Pet stores, pet supermarkets RSPCA Cats Protection Local cattery Local vet clinic
Listening to people and helping them	Probation service Police force – clerical as well as uniformed Counselling services Customer services Social worker Financial advisers Youth service
Working with children	Nurseries, playgroups Schools – teaching assistant/teacher Ground crew – childcare at airport Toy shop assistant, store manager Children's clothing stores, departmental stores with children's departments Charity organisations
Food and drink	Teaching cooking to adults at local college Selling at speciality stores, e.g. wine shop, supermarket, delicatessen Setting up own business – selling sandwiches Cordon bleu chef – cooking for businesses/dinner parties/children's parties Working in a restaurant Market researcher

Fig. 6. Matching potential employers to your interests.

Turning a hobby into a career

Do you relish an interest or hobby sufficiently enough to make a career out of it, either through starting your own business or working for somebody else? Or would you prefer to keep it for pleasure? Examples are:

I love badminton	and I'd love to teach it – I enjoy working with people of all ages. I'd enjoy doing an adult education course and seeing others get pleasure out of something I like.
I love badminton	but I couldn't teach it – I'd prefer to keep it as a hobby. It would be too much hassle to teach.
I love boats	and I sell them full time now for a dealer – so I've taken up horse riding at the weekends instead to do something different!
I love boats	but I wouldn't want to get into business with them – they are my hobby.

Trying something new

There's a wide range of courses in adult education, many of which could give you invaluable insight into a new career. You could try counselling courses, computing, cookery, languages, word processing, horticulture – you never know where they might lead:

Case study: Helen goes into teaching _____

I went back to college to refresh my computing skills. I really enjoyed the course and loved the college atmosphere – I made lots of friends and felt very much at home there. At the end of the course, my tutor asked me if I'd be interested in teaching at the college; I'd had a secretarial background before I had the children, which I think helped. I didn't want to go back to doing secretarial work, but my new career as an adult education teacher has really been just what I wanted. I've had to train for a qualification, which has been an extra boost. _____

Who or what do you want to work with?

Consider carefully what – or who – you want to spend most of your time working with:

◆ *Information and data*
   What sort of information would you like to work with? Think back to your school or college days and your current interests – what appeals to you the most? Economics, statistics, history, science, information technology, geography, mathematics, finance, art history?

◆ *Things*
   What sort of things would you like to work with? 'Things' include medicine, plants, buildings, electrics, water, air, the earth, energy, fabrics, colours, food and animals.

◆ *Ideas*
   Many people work with ideas, whether stories (novelists, for example), anything visual, business ideas, political and religious beliefs and concepts.

◆ *People*
   The possibilities are so varied that they are worth considering in more detail in the next section.

Working with people

Most jobs involve contact with people. Do you have a preferred group of people you would like to work with? Do any of these particularly make you feel, 'Yes, I'd like to help or work with them'?

the general public	children
teenagers	adults
professionals	the elderly
mentally disabled	babies
physically disabled	parents
teenage mothers	people in prison
people with learning difficulties	high flyers

the bereaved   students
the third age – those 50–70   tourists

You can work with these groups of people in a wide variety of careers sectors. What about the situations they are in?

Do you want to work with people who:	Examples of career areas:
are ill	health services, counselling
are in trouble with the law	police service, probation service, prison service, social work, youth and community work
need love and care	residential centres, day care centres, homes, hospitals
want to have fun	leisure centres, play groups, holidays, hotels, tourist information centres
want to get fit	sports teaching/coaching for schools/colleges, personal training
want advice	health visiting, counselling financial institutions, careers counselling
want to learn	schools, colleges, universities, WEA, private colleges
need a personal service	hair, beauty, massage, taxi driving, cleaning, cooking
have an emergency	ambulance driving, police service, fire service
wish to go/are on holiday	travel agencies, package tours, hotels, tourist information centres
want to plan for the future	financial adviser, funeral director, careers counsellor, insurance

wish to buy a product or service	sales staff, financial adviser, customer service assistants, insurance

Don't forget that within every career sector there will be different levels of staff, such as:

◆ support staff – clerical, administrative, secretaries/PAs, receptionists, filing clerks, wage clerks, accounting technicians, sales assistants;

◆ management staff – marketing, sales managers, finance directors, accountants, IT specialists, sales assistants;

◆ professionals – specialists in their area, e.g. doctor, vet, prison officer, financial adviser – who usually have professional qualifications in order to practise.

Depending on how much responsibility you want and how much training you are prepared to do, one of those levels of work will be more suited to you and your needs than the others.

Returning to what you used to do

If you're thinking of returning to a past career, find out what's changed in terms of the working conditions, the technology used and the training required. You may need to do a refresher course. Contact the appropriate professional organisation to find out. The careers book *Occupations*, available in your public library, lists these. Talk to people who work in the field to see what has changed and ask them if you could spend a couple of days with them to find out how reality differs from the time when you were there. Get up to date with the latest trends and thinking by reading magazines and specialist newspapers available through your newsagent or in a good reference library. Ask yourself if you want the same amount of responsibility as you had before.

Be prepared to change career

After some research, you may decide that your old career isn't right for you any more. This might be deflating, but try to work out what it was about your job that you enjoyed so much. The people you worked with? The work itself? Could another organisation offer you something similar, enabling you to put your skills and talents to good use while working in something that interests you. Many firms seek to recruit people with past experience that would be relevant to them.

However much you enjoyed your last spell of paid employment with the employer you were once with, you've moved on since. What you originally enjoyed doing so much may have lost its appeal and you think to yourself 'I couldn't do this any more!' Don't fall victim to thinking 'but I can't do anything else.' *You can.* You can learn to do something else by re-training and studying for a new career!

Refreshing your skills

If you are planning a move back into a similar line of work, a refresher course on your CV will show an employer that you are motivated, up to date and serious about your job hunting. It will also boost your confidence, may give you some work experience and may lead to a job – all things which will add to your ability to 'hit the ground running'. If you were involved in a profession, contact your professional body to see if refresher courses are available for those returning to work.

Thinking about career choices

Here are some further ideas to kick off. (They are listed here according to the Careers Library Classification Index – see page 92 for details of how to use the CLCI system in a careers library.) You may look at some categories and think, 'Yes, that sounds interesting', while for others you might say to yourself, 'Forget it!'

A Self-Employment
B Armed Forces
C Administration, Business, Clerical
E Art and Design
F Teaching and Cultural Activities
G Entertainment and Leisure
I Hospitality, Catering and Other Services

J   Health and Medical Services
K   Social and Related Services
L   Law and Related Work
M   Security and Protective Services
N   Finance and Related Work
O   Buying, Selling and Related Services
Q   Science, Mathematics and Related Work
R   Engineering
S   Manufacturing Industries
U   Construction and Land Services
W   Animals, Plants and Nature
Y   Transport
(Note that the letters D, H, P, T, V, X and Z are not used in
the Index.)

You may have a natural leaning towards some of these; there
are a whole range of jobs in each sector, all requiring different
levels of qualification and all demanding certain skills and
qualities. As you discovered when you worked through the
exercises in Chapter 5, they all require skills in the key areas of:

◆   managing yourself
◆   showing you can deliver (customer care)
◆   communication skills (with customers and colleagues)
◆   carrying out routine work
◆   working in a team
◆   basic skills (in numeracy and literacy).

Some jobs will put more emphasis on particular skills than on
others. Most jobs will, of course, demand different levels of
knowledge, expertise and training once you get away from the
transferable skills and into the nitty gritty of the job. These are
things you can learn or be taught, either by taking a course or
by training on the job, perhaps through a work experience
placement.

Careers for the mature person

Many careers are ideal for people who have done something
else first, so they then have more experience of life and can
empathise with a greater number of customers from a wider

spread of backgrounds. Some of these are:

financial advisory services	hotel management
careers services	local government
retail	teaching English
libraries	the church
legal services	animal care
introductory agencies	funeral services
house-sitting	transportation
teaching	media
museums	social services
insurance	police services
health care	personal services
probation service	management
working with children	working with the elderly

Many of these careers have vocational courses which you can work towards and in some instances, if you have already been working in a voluntary capacity, you may be able to claim credit for your past knowledge and experience based on the system called Accreditation of Prior Learning. Chapter 9 explains more, but it works on the basis that there is no point in relearning what you already know.

Late entry advice

If you consult the book *Occupations* in any careers library, you will see that under each job is a section for 'late entry'. This gives advice to the non-school leaver considering the career. Follow the further information avenues as well – you could contact the professional body to see what their advice would be to you as a woman returner.

> Remember, many employers favour people with experience of life.

Expanding and new careers

If you can acquire a job or career in an expanding area, you will increase your chances of getting work and remaining employed. Go into an area of work which is decreasing in opportunity and you increase your chances of being out of a job.

Where are the lost jobs? These are chiefly in lower skilled plant and machine operating, single skilled construction work, unskilled occupations, manual occupations and single skilled/ semi-skilled jobs in manufacturing.

Find out about your local area

Find out from your local LSC which sectors are expanding in your area, and whether they have any knowledge of local firms which are particularly supportive to women returners or mature employees. They will also be able to give you data about business opportunities in your area.

Sectors on the way up are: business services, financial services, advisory work of any capacity, insurance, IT, law, leisure, recruitment, recreation, tourism, retail, wholesale distribution, hotels, catering and the business service sector – health, public administration and so on.

Getting in touch with new careers

There have been a number of new careers which have burst forth onto the careers scene, either thanks to advances in technology or social changes. Some of these are:

- counselling
- complementary health medicine
- careers planning/life planning
- financial advising
- science, technology
- health and fitness
- crime prevention, security
- personal services such as hair and beauty, cleaning
- call centres and direct telephone services
- information technology
- anything involving animals
- multi-skilled work.

If you were to have looked through a careers book a few years ago, you might not have seen these.

Try it now	◆ List your interests.
	◆ Refer to the *Yellow Pages* and make a list of all those companies which match your interests.
	◆ Find out what sort of people they recruit by going to the careers section of your local library.

Summary

You should by now start to have an idea of the sort of job you're looking for – the next chapter will show you how to do your research.

◆ Think as broadly as you can when you are thinking about your future career – think laterally. Focus first on the area or sector you would like to work in (e.g. leisure industry, education), and then work out the job you would like to do within it (e.g. fitness trainer, teacher).

◆ Remember that the more interested you are in the products and services your company is offering, the better a job you are likely to do.

◆ Think carefully about running your own business. Talk to people who are doing it already. Get their advice.

CHAPTER 8

Researching Your Future

T he next stage is to find out more about the areas of work
which interest you. Of key importance will be the amount
of training you are prepared to put in and what the job
opportunities are in your local area, because you may need to
be more flexible than you originally hoped. The good news is
that there is plenty of information available, in printed material
and electronically, on the Internet.

Researching your career interests

Some employers say there is little point in going to the library
to read up about the career you have in mind, because things
change so quickly that anything you read is certain to be out of
date. In the next breath, they would express surprise and
disappointment if you hadn't made an effort to read everything
you can lay your hands on about the work you are planning to
do and the company you plan to do it with.

The careers library

The careers section in the library is organised under a system
called the CLCI, the 'Careers Library Classification Index'. Each
career sector is filed under a letter of the alphabet and the
different careers filed within that class (see pages 87–88). Thus,
anything to do with finance is under the letter N, banking is a
further subdivision under NAD. Go along to the library and
learn how to use the system. There will be someone there who
can explain it further to you.

The book *Occupations* will also be there; it goes through
each sector in turn, describing the jobs available within it,
covering the work, the work environment, skills and interests,
entry requirements, training, pay and conditions, prospects,
and further reading. The three sections which will be of

particular use to you will be the advice on late entry; the section on related opportunities which suggests other careers you might want to consider which are similar; and further information with addresses to contact.

Usefully, if you're not a whiz at using the Internet, it gives web-site addresses of the professional bodies for each career, enabling you to go straight to the heart of the matter without searching randomly.

Check out too your local government web-site, because there'll certainly be information on the local labour market, training programmes, careers services, ideas on the sort of help available for those seeking to run their own business, and re-training opportunities. To find your local government web-site, put in the name of your county and ask the computer to search, or get the web address by calling the local authority.

Researching the sector

Try to find out as much as you can about the sector you propose to work in. You need to know that you'll be happy working alongside your colleagues, that you'll fit in well and that you have a natural interest in it. There are a number of ways you can do this.

Contact professional bodies

Most professions have a ruling body which sets down the standards and behaviour expected of their members and which also lays down the structure and content of the training required to join their ranks. Professional bodies are a useful source of information, and you can either write for details or visit their web-sites. Usefully, increasing numbers are producing advice for people who are changing career and seeking to enter their profession later on in life.

Study the trade and professional magazines

You don't have to subscribe to professional or trade magazines which will keep you up to date with current trends in your chosen career area. Your local library will have many of these and will also have business reference books listing companies in your area which are relevant to you.

Make time to read the professional and trade magazines which concern the area of commerce or industry you're looking at. There may be hints on applying for jobs in them, but there will certainly be comment on anything topical which you may be asked about in interview, or failing that, which you can comment on yourself. It will be important to show on your CV and at interview that you're up to date with developments in the industry.

Study newspapers

They too will comment on the issues of the day, particularly if they offer a daily supplement relating to a career area. An example is the *Guardian* which covers 'Media' on Monday, 'Education' on Tuesday, 'Social and Community Services' on Wednesday, 'Science and Engineering' on Thursday. If you're not interested in reading up what's happening in the news in your sector, then it probably isn't for you.

Using recruitment agencies

Recruitment agencies can offer you considerable insight into job opportunities in a given sector without you even leaving home, if you have access to the Internet. Companies such as Reed and Stepstone both have considerable web-sites, offering a huge amount of information for those seeking work, including advice on how to write a CV, cope with interviews and salary checks. Many larger agencies offer specialist sections so that you can really get a good idea of what is on offer in the particular sector you wish to work in. They also have vacancies on-line whereby you can check out what's on offer in your part of the country, and some specialise in placing older workers. Make sure the company is a member of the professional body for recruitment agencies, the Recruitment and Employment Confederation. Recruitment companies should not charge you for signing on to their books.

Finding out about companies

You can find out which companies operate in the sector you

want to work in, and in your area, by checking the *Yellow Pages*, or going to your local government's regional web-site and doing a company search there, for example, by typing the word 'florist' in if you want to become a florist. Once you have a list of companies which relate to your career plans, you can start to research them.

Going directly to a company

Many companies have a web-site – don't be put off by how small the company is, as many see it as a useful way to achieve an immediate global reach. Company web-sites can give you lots of useful information, such as:

- ◆ an introduction to the company, usually on a page called 'About us' or something similar
- ◆ a history of the company
- ◆ the management structure – useful to see how many women are on the board and at the top
- ◆ the products and services it provides
- ◆ an outline of the vision for the future
- ◆ news and press releases
- ◆ lots of financial information
- ◆ details on the location of the company
- ◆ a guide to its ethics and values, which you may need to read between the lines
- ◆ initiatives it may have introduced to help employees at work, such as moves to help staff achieve a work–life balance
- ◆ documents such as the Annual Report
- ◆ a links page to other relevant sites
- ◆ a contact-us section
- ◆ a page for recruitment, describes perhaps as 'Jobs', 'Work for us!', 'Recruitment', 'Careers', with information on how to apply.

Some may even have a chat page, where you can make contact with staff already working for the company; others offer you the chance to do a test to see if you're the sort of person who would fit in well. Employee profiles are a frequent feature, although one has to read between the lines – no company is going to have a profile of a disgruntled employee on its pages.

The old type of personnel department has been replaced in many organisations by human resources departments, involved in recruiting, training and developing staff to meet the needs of the organisation and its future. Where they exist, personnel departments are more likely to deal with straight recruitment. Training departments organise training programmes for staff designed to meet the needs of an organisation. Human resource, and personnel departments may be able to send you careers information if it is produced by the company.

Attend careers fairs

Many companies attend recruitment fairs, organised by local careers services. They go because they want to meet prospective recruits, so it's a useful time to dress the part and take your CV along. Go with a good idea of what you want to achieve from the event, whether it's information about different careers, what companies are doing to help women returners, or making contacts you can go back to at a later stage. At the very least, career fairs provide an opportunity for you to meet representatives from different companies and see how their organisations 'fit' with your goals, values and needs. For example, some company values may particularly appeal to you, perhaps because they believe in a sensible work–life balance, or they promote family-friendly policies (find out how), or seek to protect the environment.

Visit them

If a company has a show room, pop in and visit to see what impression you get of the staff and working surroundings provided for them, especially if there is an area open to the public. Do the staff look happy and motivated? Are they keen to help? Do you feel you could work happily with them? What do they like about working for the organisation?

Check out the press

What is happening to the company in the news? Search the local and national press for anything which is affecting the sectors which interest you, and use any news you can see as a hook to write a letter with your CV. If a company has received a major contract, they may be seeking to recruit staff. What is one company's downfall may be another's opportunity: the company laying off staff could provide business for a careers counsellor. She could offer her services to the management to help those who have been made redundant find work.

Running your own business

If you are thinking of running your own business, it's particularly important that you know your local area well, because then you're in a better position to spot what's missing. Inspiration may suddenly come to you as you walk down the high street, thinking 'What we really need is a ...' or overhear a conversation on a bus, 'There's no one who does this, any more. It's such a shame.' Look for hints and suggestions from the public themselves by overhearing conversations discreetly, talking to friends and family and other people you know. Somewhere, an idea may come up for you to follow up and research.

Checking out the competition

You may have liked the idea of working at one particular company and so ignored its competitors. Don't! It's worth doing thorough research because you might come up with something that surprises you. Find out from *Yellow Pages* who the main competitors are – and rummage around to find out what you can about them. They may offer a higher starting wage/better holidays or have more exciting expansion plans for the area.

> **Don't put all your eggs in one basket!**

Considering some vital questions

As part of your research, try to talk informally with as many professionals as you can – personnel departments, recruitment consultants, careers librarians, friends who run their own businesses. Some key questions are shown below (and some you need to ask yourself, too):

◆ How can you train to become a ... and how long will it take? (Am I prepared to spend this amount of time training?)

◆ Is it possible to do this sort of work from home? (Can I organise myself and my family sufficiently to cope?)

◆ Can I do this on a part-time basis? (Will it provide sufficient income for my needs?)

◆ What sorts of skills and qualities do you need in this line of work? (Do I have them? If not, how can I develop them?)

◆ What are the advantages of entering the profession through this route? And the disadvantages? (How do I feel about these?)

◆ Who are the main employers in my home area? (Are they expanding or downsizing?)

◆ What do people tend to enjoy most about working in this line of career? (Does it also appeal to me?)

◆ How did you establish your own business? (Have I got what it takes?)

◆ Is this a sector which is very competitive and for which I'll need to get some work experience to increase my chances of landing a job?

◆ Is there any chance of my doing a few days' work shadowing, so that I can get a better idea of what this job involves?

Make use of your network

Ask everyone you know whether they know of anyone who:
◆ might be hiring staff
◆ could provide you with information
◆ could tell you about this course
◆ has got in this way
◆ is expanding
◆ could advise you on your CV
◆ could offer you work experience.

Understanding how career paths have changed

In the old days, you chose one career and usually stuck with it.

Now things have changed. People are changing career four or
five times in their working lives and will have periods of time
when they dip into episodes of:

◆ permanent employment
◆ part-time work
◆ re-training
◆ underemployment
◆ study
◆ travel
◆ personal time out to achieve goals
◆ maternity/paternity leave
◆ temporary work
◆ unemployment.

This has forced education and training providers, governments
and employers to change the way they think about the people
they recruit, and to be more flexible about the entry routes into
work. The fact that many skills now transfer between one job
and another has facilitated this development, and made life
easier for those seeking to switch careers or re-enter the
workplace.

One person, several careers

Although people may switch careers, they are probably related
in that they demand the same skills, interests and qualities. A
nurse might change her career to become a counsellor or work
for a health promotion unit. She could also teach student
nurses, or enter management, sales or personnel.

These careers share similar skills, qualities and interests.
They demand skills in communicating with a wide variety of
people, often under pressure and in sensitive situations. The
post-holders must be able to gain the confidence of others, to
advise their customers and to share information with them in a
way that they will understand. Such careers require the ability
to pay close attention to detail, insight into human nature and
the ability to keep records. They call for patience, tact and
tenacity. They also cater for people who have a strong interest
in health, psychology and helping others.

What does this mean for the individual?

It will be more important than ever to have a strong sense of:

◆ career and life decision-making skills, as the two become ever closely linked

◆ the importance and willingness to learn new skills and to keep up to date with technology

◆ your own worth in the job market

◆ change

◆ how to find work and present yourself rapidly to future employers.

At the moment, you are simply seeking to go out to work. Once you are there, give yourself a period in which to settle down to the job, and then spend some time thinking about these points.

Try it now

◆ Come up with a full list of all those organisations you might apply to.

◆ Find out more information about their products and services – if they have a showroom or a sales room, visit it to see what you think.

◆ Read what you can about the current trends affecting that industry.

Summary

Career paths have changed tremendously in the last two decades and consequently it's important to keep up with technology developments and new careers.

◆ Semi-skilled and unskilled jobs have reduced in number; the professions, managerial and skilled posts are on the rise.

◆ There's no such thing as a job for life (except that of being a parent) or job security any more.

CHAPTER 9

The most important requirements for successful study are enthusiasm and determination

Starting Back Through Study

I f the thought of going back into the classroom fills you with absolute horror, then rest assured: adult education is very different from school. Firstly, adults attend through choice – they want to be there. Secondly, classes are more informal and relaxed. For example, many institutions run courses for one day, simply to offer a taster of a subject for those who are interested in it. Thirdly, you can learn at home, either by correspondence courses or on-line.

You should also know that there is far more emphasis on learning by doing these days. Consequently your past experiences can frequently be taken into account when you are about to enrol on a course.

> **Many courses allow mature students with appropriate experience to join courses without the formal entry requirements demanded of younger people.**

Where can I study?

There is a whole range of educational providers throughout the country, including:

- colleges of further education
- tertiary colleges
- colleges of higher education
- universities (there are no polytechnics now)
- adult community colleges
- WEA classes for adults
- private colleges (usually more expensive)
- the Open University
- correspondence courses with organisations such as the National Extension College
- opening learning courses – you train with the aid of course

materials, videos, computer packages, audio tapes and the Internet.

They all provide prospectuses free of charge outlining their courses, facilities, fees, dates and contact numbers for further information. Call the main number to ask for one; you can find this in *Yellow Pages* or by looking in your local paper where they may advertise. Your local library will also have leaflets of local and national providers, including university prospectuses.

You can also find out information about each of these at your local careers service company or your LSC. If you live in a rural area, you could take a distance learning or correspondence course. The free helpline called Learn Direct will help you find the course you want nearest you (see Useful Addresses). You have a number of sources of information available to you on the Internet, and in your local library and careers services to help you pinpoint the right institution and the right course for you. Many web-sites have search engines, enabling you to find the right institution and the right course. This chapter will help point you to the right web pages to aid you further.

These providers will have advisers who will help you determine which course is the best one for you, bearing in mind when you last studied, the level of education you have obtained already, and your future career aspirations. Don't forget that many have advisory centres specifically to help students over 21. Contact them as entry requirements to courses are frequently waived for adults.

Provision is also made to support students with special needs, such as dyslexia. Let the institution know what your needs are and what sort of support you require from them and they will do what they can to help you.

Things to think about when choosing your course

- ◆ What do you want to study? For how long? At what level?
- ◆ How do you learn best? By doing? Watching others and then doing it yourself? Studying the theory and then putting theory into practice?

- ◆ Where do you want to learn? Do you want to attend classes in person in your area? Or are you happy to learn over the Internet at home?
- ◆ What do you want to get out of a course? A qualification? Something career related?

What about cost?

There is a charge for most courses, although many colleges offer concessionary fees to those on a Job Seeker's allowance, or who are receiving means-tested benefits, or are self-employed or over 60. If you are studying something which is directly related to a job, you could apply for a Career Development Loan (see Useful Addresses) which could cover courses fees and other costs such as books, materials and childcare. If you are studying for a course which leads to a National Vocational Qualification, you should be able to get tax relief.

Before you enrol on a course, you should check whether there will be any additional costs you will need to provide for to cover things such as field courses, particular books or equipment.

If you run into problems paying for a course talk to the Finance Office as soon as you can. They will do what they can to help you.

Looking at higher education

Higher National Diplomas, degrees and postgraduate courses all constitute higher education. There are some 42,000 courses to choose from – those of an academic nature (e.g. history, English literature, chemistry) and vocational ones (e.g. information technology, hotel management). The UCAS website itself has a very useful section specifically dedicated to mature students.

Accessing higher education

Access courses offer mature students a qualification which will enable them to proceed to a higher education course. They may be full or part time and their length will depend accordingly: usually they are either one or two years in length. All courses have core subjects including study skills, life skills and maths, all of which will ensure that you have the necessary foundation skills for successful study. You also choose an area to specialise in, depending on your interests, your careers aspirations and what is available at that college. Social sciences, media studies, humanities, languages, health, science and sport, dance and music may be some of the subjects on offer.

Many adults study GCSEs and A levels part time, perhaps because a university requires students to have a particular A level in order to start a degree subject. Most courses are one or two years.

Degrees

Get in touch with your nearest university or college of higher education and ask for a prospectus. When you read through it, you will get an idea of the really enormous range of courses on offer. Set up a meeting with the Mature Students' Office (or Adult Continuing Education Centre – names vary) and discuss your choices with an adviser.

If you are thinking about signing up for a degree, consider:

◆ What are your reasons for entering higher education?
◆ What difference will it make to your job prospects? (The university's career service will be able to help you there.)
◆ Would you be better suited to study for a degree part time or full time?
◆ Are you prepared to commit yourself to several years of study?
◆ How will you fund it? Full-time students have to contribute up to £1,000 annually towards their tuition fees, depending on the income of their spouse or parents.
◆ How do you want to be assessed?
◆ Do you want to stick to one subject, or combine two or three?

If you can study anywhere in the country, take a look at the UCAS web-site which details courses in further and higher education and gives lots of advice about their entry requirements.

The Credit Accumulation and Transfer system (CATs for short) allows students to move from one college to another without having to start another course from scratch. This may be especially useful if you have to move halfway through the course because your partner has to change job location.

Work-related qualifications

Within the remit of higher education, but worth a mention as a work-related course, come Higher National Diplomas/ Certificates (HNDs/HNCs). These are two- or three-year courses of a vocational nature, in business studies or leisure and tourism, for example. General National Vocational Qualifications (GNVQs) are the work-related courses A levels and GCSEs. They incorporate study in core skills, such as application of number, information technology and communication skills, but then they specialise in fields such as:

Art and Design	Business Studies
Construction and Built Environment	Leisure, Tourism and Travel
	Health and Social Care
Engineering	Information Technology
Media	

There are three levels of GNVQ, called Foundation, Intermediate and Advanced. They take one to two years to complete and provide a foundation for employment, further and higher education, depending on the level. Talk to an adviser at the college to determine which level is right for you.

Training for a job

You can train for specific careers by studying at college or even at home, depending on how practical the course is. The following list is included to show the breadth of career courses educational providers may offer:

accounting	business administration
retail distribution	computer literacy
electrical installation	hairdressing

body massage

nursery nursing

legal studies

sports coaching

manufacturing

media studies

science

counselling

financial services

art and design

blockwork/brickwork

civil engineering

customer care

electronics

food preparation

hospitality management

inn-keeping

massage

journalism

tourism

insurance

agriculture

equine studies

aromatherapy

surveying

complementary therapies

desktop publishing

furniture restoration

printmaking

word processing

health and holistic therapies

teaching English

tour operator's certificate

management

marketing

motor vehicle repairs

social work

teaching adult education

animal care

beauty therapy

health care

computing/information
   technology

interior decorating

engineering

gardening

food hygiene

licensed trade

creative writing

plumbing

return to learning

teacher training

banking

horticulture

dog grooming

architecture

book-keeping

picture framing and mounting

office skills

Building on the example shown in Figure 6 (p. 82), Figure 7 adds in some of the courses likely to provide qualifications related to particular interest areas.

Increasing numbers of people want to study short, intensive courses and so many colleges offer work-related subjects at weekends. Ask your college for a list of part-time, short courses – these are constantly being updated.

My interests	Organisations that match those interests	Suitable courses
Cats	Pet stores, pet supermarkets RSPCA Cats Protection Local cattery Local vet clinic	Animal care Information technology Customer service Retail and distribution
Listening to people and helping them	Probation service Police force – clerical as well as uniformed Counselling services Customer services Social worker Financial advisers Youth service	Health and social care Customer service Introduction to counselling Diploma in Social Work Financial services
Working with children	Nurseries, playgroups Schools – teaching assistant/ teacher Ground crew – childcare at airport Toy shop assistant, store manager Children's clothing stores, departmental stores with children's departments Charity organisations	NNEB – Nursery Nursing Diploma Introduction to working with children Retail and distribution Customer service First Aid course Supervisory management
Food and drink	Teaching cooking to adults at local college Selling at speciality stores, e.g. wine shop, supermarket, delicatessen Setting up own business – selling sandwiches Cordon bleu chef Working in a restaurant Market researcher	Setting up in business Retail and distribution Customer service Wine appreciation course Food hygiene certificate Book-keeping Adult Education Certificate

Fig. 7. Matching your interests to vocational qualifications.

Examples of part-time courses found at a typical further education college included:

◆ RSA Certificate for Part-time Youth Workers (you have to work with young people aged 11+ for one session a week)
◆ Introduction to Counselling
◆ Teacher/Trainer Diplomas
◆ Certificate of Higher Education (Supported Learning) for learning support staff (classroom assistants, welfare assistants, playgroup and play workers)
◆ Short courses for those seeking to work with the elderly, e.g. Ageing Process and Illness, Moving and Handling
◆ Private Secretary's Certificate
◆ Beauty Therapy
◆ Diploma in Reflexology
◆ Introduction to Management.

Many such career courses are relatively short, although it is, of course, possible to study longer for a related degree or HND at a higher education institute.

Since many courses are taught in units, it is frequently possible to study those units which will go towards fulfilling your career aspirations without taking the entire diploma or course. A further development within the educational and training systems has been that of National Vocational Qualifications, which can be taken in units.

Getting to grips with NVQs/SVQs

National Vocational Qualifications (NVQs, or SVQs in Scotland) are based on standards set by leading bodies representing employers. They are designed to meet the needs of particular industries, so they are very relevant to the workplace. You should have some full- or part-time employment or be involved in some relevant charity work to acquire an NVQ, although you may be able to achieve credit towards a qualification if your past learning is assessed – the next section deals with that.

How they work

There are five levels of NVQ:

Level	Type of work
5	Professional, chartered, senior management roles.
4	Technical and junior management occupations.
3	Technician, craft, skilled, supervisory occupations.
2/3	Operative/semi-skilled occupations.
1	Foundation skills. Mostly routine and predictable work.

An NVQ is broken down into bits. Taking Business Administration as an example, the units you are assessed in might include:

◆ Communicating information
◆ Data processing
◆ Stock handling
◆ Mail handling
◆ Reprographics
◆ Liaising with callers and colleagues
◆ Health and safety
◆ Creating and maintaining business relationships.

Each unit will be broken down into different elements; for example, within 'creating and maintaining business relationships' you might have a number of activities you have to prove you can do, such as creating and maintaining business relationships with other members of staff or developing positive relationships with customers. Each would have a number of core activities you would need to undertake at a set standard, such as:

◆ requests from your colleagues for help are dealt with promptly and willingly;
◆ information is passed on to your colleagues promptly and accurately;
◆ when you seek assistance, you do so politely.

Your assessor would look at the evidence you have collected to prove you can do these things – or, indeed, watch you in action

– to assess whether you have met the standard required.

If you were doing a level 1 qualification, the sort of tasks you could have to do would be far simpler than if you were doing level 5. Your level would be determined by the sort of job you were in already or the range of experience you already had.

After you have worked your way through the units (many of the tasks can be done simultaneously in the course of the day's activities), you acquire an NVQ in Business Administration. Past experience in voluntary activities may give you a head start!

What do employers think?

Many employers are still trying to come to grips with NVQs. They dislike the paperwork involved (so do many of the students). However, many employers also found that NVQs increased the productivity of people, motivated them, and also helped in recruiting – they knew what applicants could do if they had an NVQ.

At the end of September 1997, 2.5 million people had either gained an NVQ or an SVQ or were working towards one. Most of them were over 24 and employed.

Taking past learning into account

The Accreditation of Prior Learning and Achievement system is based on the sensible principle that, if somebody knows how to do something already, there is absolutely no point in them learning how to do it all over again. That is a waste of time.

So you may find that you have already mastered the skills and knowledge necessary to acquire some NVQs/SVQs because the system takes into account your past experience and knowledge. In other words you can get credit for what you have already learned, no matter where, how or with whom you learned it. So how does the system work? Figure 8 shows you the steps involved.

You can acquire APL for a very wide variety of skills and competencies, such as answering the telephone and directing telephone calls; organising yourself and others; preparing and writing reports and routine letters. You may have learned or done these things at home, doing voluntary work in any

Identify the area you want to get credit for
e.g. information technology

↓

Match your strengths with the requirements of the
qualification or training programme you want to do e.g. look at
everything you know that you can do relating to information technology

↓

Get proof that you can do the things you actually say you can do
e.g. creating your own documents by displaying evidence of
your work in a folder

↓

An assessor who is an expert in the area you want to get credit for
assesses your work i.e. to make sure that it matches the expected standard

↓

He or she will either give you credit for the work, or explain where you
need to gain more evidence or further your skills, based on whether your
evidence is relevant, authentic, current and sufficient

↓

You undertake further study in the workplace or by doing voluntary work

↓

You gain an NVQ/SVQ unit or element of competence

Fig. 8. How to get credit for what you can already do.

capacity, or on work experience. Find out if your local college
has an APL adviser and set up a meeting.

> **You may find that you're able to pick up a qualification
> faster than you thought, thanks to your past experiences.**

Studying at home

A number of universities and colleges are beginning to offer
courses on a correspondence or distance learning basis. The
Open University, for example, offers a wide range of courses,
from arts and humanities to health and social welfare, and
from business and management to the environment. These run
from February to October and have no entry requirements.

Although the Open University is based in Milton Keynes, it has 13 regional centres around the UK which provide advice and guidance to prospective students. For more information contact the OU direct (see Useful Addresses). The University of London offers an external degree scheme in arts and humanities subjects.

Studying with a correspondence college

The Association of British Correspondence Courses (see Useful Addresses) will send you a list of organisations which may be able to help you. The National Extension College is one example of a major provider of distance-learning courses, many of which are career related. There is no academic year as such – you can usually start when you like. You receive your course material after you have signed up and you work your way through it at your own pace, sending in assignments for marking and receiving comments back from your own personal tutor. Most colleges are happy for you to ring up if you have any difficulties and also to give advice on the phone about the course which is best for you.

> **Entry requirements will vary depending on the course but enthusiasm and determination are vital!**

Some correspondence courses will prepare you for exams, such as GCSEs and A Levels, which you may sit at a local college. However, you don't have to sign up for an exam class – you can do anything that interests you, from gardening (leisure) to animal grooming, short story writing, women in management, tourism and classical studies. Fees vary from college to college, depending on the course and the support you receive.

Become an e-learner!

Why not become an e-learner? (Imagine explaining that to your friends.) You can do so on an informal basis by surfing the Internet to boost your knowledge of something you particularly want to know about. If, for example, you wanted to get information on how to handle a teenager whom you suspected was taking drugs, and you searched the Internet for advice, then you would be an informal e-learner. Alternatively, you can follow more formal e-learning where a provider has set out a course of topics for you to study.

The advantage of e-learning is that you can learn at your own pace when it suits you. The disadvantage is that it can be impersonal and lonely, and you may prefer a learning option which will get you out of the house. It has to be said that a big plus of learning at a college is that tutors should have strong links with employers who may see the course you're on as a way to recruit new trainees.

Juggling family demands and study

You'll need somewhere quiet to study and you'll need to find the time of day which suits you best. Some people find they can achieve a lot by getting up early in the mornings while everybody else is in bed and distractions are at a minimum. Find the right time for you when your brain power feels at its most productive.

You will find that, as well as a library, most colleges will have a huge information technology resource, including a flexible learning centre where you can go and sit down and work through things at your own pace. There will also be resources for the study of media, languages, travel and beauty and hairdressing. Don't feel overwhelmed by it all. Take advantage of any 'tours of the college facilities' provided – many tutors do this themselves on the first day.

What about childcare?

Many institutions offer some form of childcare, but places go very quickly so if you need childcare the sooner you check about this, the better. Some courses are actually time-tabled to take place during school hours.

What if the course isn't right for me?

Some people will begin a course and find as the weeks progress that the course simply isn't right for them. If this is the case, you should talk to your tutor and then to those in charge of registering students to see if there is a more appropriate class for you to switch to, as Nicola did:

Case study: Nicola studying French _____

I enrolled for French but by the second week I knew I was struggling. I spoke to my tutor and then the Adult Registration team. I thought they might tell me just to keep on trying, but in fact the lady on the other end of the phone listened carefully and then said. 'Well, the important thing about adult education is that you should enjoy it – we must find you another course at a different level.' I swapped to a lower level, where I'm coping better and enjoying myself!' _____

> **Remember – learning should be fun!**

Try it now
- Identify courses which will move your career plans forward.
- Find out where you can study them and which courses are available by calling Learn Direct or visiting its web-site; or going to the UCAS web-site if you want to do a course in higher education.
- Get lots of information on the course – see if the course tutor has anything in addition to the prospectus.
- Find out what the application process is.
- Apply and start. Good luck!

Summary

Adult education classes have expanded considerably due to the government's efforts to encourage everyone to make lifelong learning a goal.
- There are all sorts of courses at many different levels; somewhere, you will find a course to suit your needs.
- Extra help may be available if you have particular learning difficulties or special needs.
- Mature students make very good students because they are committed and motivated to learn and they study through choice.

*Show employers
you've kept in
touch with
what's going on*

CHAPTER 10

Getting Up to Date with the Workplace

The government has tried to encourage business growth and expansion throughout the UK in the last decade. One of the initiatives spearheading this effort was the formation of a group of bodies throughout the UK called Training and Enterprise Councils in England and Wales (TECs); these have now been replaced by Learning and Skills Councils, but they have introduced numerous initiatives to help people return to work.

Boosting your computer skills

> **All jobs are touched by information technology one way or another.**

You cannot avoid computers in the modern workplace. As a result, there are lots of courses provided by educational establishments throughout the country, both private and local authority.

Courses will cover a range of student needs, including:

◆ the complete and absolute beginner
◆ those seeking to update their skills because the world of technology has left them behind
◆ those wishing to change career and who need a qualification in this area to do so
◆ those wishing to advance their IT careers further.

Absolute beginner classes usually go at a very gentle pace so that you can study at a speed which suits you and they try to be as jargon-free as possible. These often have titles like 'Computing for the Bewildered'. They are not going to consist of any Bill Gates types – although you'll always get one who is faster than everyone else. The rest of you will unite in sympathy!

You can learn about and use some or all of the following:

- the keyboard and short cuts
- word processing
- databases
- coding and programming
- Visual Basic projects
- desktop publishing
- Powerpoint
- computer aided design
- Excel.

These skills will enhance your job prospects in the employment market. Talk to people you know at work and find out when and how they might be used.

You can study on your own

Open learning (often called flexible learning) enables you to study at your own pace when you want. For example, you could learn how to use a word processor, to do spreadsheets and use data software through open learning. This could lead to nationally recognised examinations. Contact your local college to see what they can do to help.

Case study: Susan studies IT at the library

Susan was impressed by the range of learning opportunities available – in her local library!

'I saw this woman sitting down at a computer – she was about my age, working away intently, I wondered what she was doing, so I looked over her shoulder. She spotted me watching her and explained she was doing a word processing course because she thought it might help get a job and because she wanted to know how to do it, anyway. I asked where her tutor was – and she told me she was teaching herself with the aid of a computer training programme. I couldn't believe it. She let me watch her for a while – I thought if she can do that, so can I, so I signed up for 15 hours to start with and soon got hooked.'

Talk to an adviser at your local college

They will talk to you about the experience you've had with computers and recommend the best class for you. This may be held during the day or one evening a week.

There's always help at hand

Don't let the IT element of a job worry you unduly.
Computers do go wrong from time to time, as you'll know
from the number of times you've rung a number for
information and the person at the other end of the line says,
'Oh, I'm sorry, we can't give you those details right now – the
computer's down'. Most companies have IT departments who
will have a help desk staffed by people ready to assist you when
your computer crashes (won't work, to you and me).

> **Don't feel embarrassed about asking for help.**

I once remember calling an office's helpline in a panic because
I couldn't get my computer to print. The chap from the IT
department came along and kindly and without any degree of
sarcasm suggested I plug the printer in at the wall ...

Learning about different equipment at work

Most offices these days have a wide range of equipment which
are common to all. These will include a fax machine,
photocopier, computers which may or may not give you access
to the Internet but will enable you to email messages, memos
or letters to colleagues or customers. Then there will also be
specialist equipment, depending on the environment you'll be
working in. It's useful if you can learn how to use this prior to
applying for a job, so that you'll be able to hit the ground
running when you arrive.

Do you know how, when and where the following pieces of
equipment or systems work, and the impact they might have
on the business and the working day?

- fax machine
- email
- photocopier
- overhead projector
- word processor
- the Internet
- a database system
- Powerpoint
- Excel.

Enrolling for a training programme

To make the most of the human resources available to enhance the country's competitiveness the government is developing many programmes to help people back into work. At the time of writing, the government's Welfare to Work strategy, for example, has created opportunities for all sorts of people to go back to work. The idea is to close the gap between the skills employers need and those which job seekers have. Most of these will have a particular slant: for example, there are New Deal programmes running for people over 50, lone parents, those with disabilities and individuals seeking to run their own business. Your local Job Centre will be able to give you a very good overview of any opportunities running in your area, and an adviser will help you pinpoint the most appropriate one for you.

Training programmes may offer you a number of elements including:

(a) short term training to give you the skills you need for interview or to redevelop your skills for a specific job;

(b) job placements – to give you an introduction to the company and the job, which may lead to a permanent job and/or full pay;

(c) training leading to NVQs.

These programmes may be particularly useful if you are feeling very nervous about going back to work; you will receive plenty of support from your adviser and the employer.

The advantage of a training programme is that it provides an opportunity for you to get your foot in the door and show what you can do. Employment on Trial, and Work Trials are two such opportunities which give the individual a chance to try out the job and see how they fit into the company; they give the company time to see how you get on.

New Deal for lone parents

The government is making efforts to help lone parents back to work. One scheme designed to help is the New Deal (which also has a section for young people). A personal adviser will meet you and discuss your plans – while giving you careers advice, they will advise you on in-work benefits and help you find suitable childcare. You can also check with your local council for a list of registered childcare providers.

'There's a high unemployment rate in my area'

Find out what local training opportunities are available from your Job Centre or local LSC – then at least you can start getting experience and training in a career area of interest. Your LSC may already be doing something to create employment opportunities in the area.

Alternatively, there may be work you can do at home, which you could train for either at the local college or by correspondence course. You could also offer your services voluntarily to a company – then when things get better they might offer you a post, even if they can't at the moment. In the meantime, watch the local press carefully for any news of any companies expanding or setting up in the area; you can then contact those companies direct to see whether they might be interested in hiring you.

Getting work experience

What's it really like at work? If you haven't been in paid employment for a long time, it is worth putting your toe back in the water, both from the point of view of testing whether a particular career is for you by watching somebody else do it (work shadowing) or by simply getting your hands dirty and seeing if you can help out at a company for a few days (work experience).

A number of courses may include the opportunity to go out on work experience and thus put into practice the skills you've learned in the classroom, especially if they are of a work-related nature. This provides a very useful opportunity to get back in touch with the workplace, but also to make contact with an employer who might offer you a job, if impressed with your work and attitude.

Work shadowing

If you've got kids, the chances are that they'll have done a period of work experience in school. The whole point of the initial work-experience stint is to give youngsters an idea of what lies behind the workplace so that they get to grips with the appropriate behaviour there and a 'feel' for what work is like. You may not have heard so much about work shadowing, but it runs alongside the work-experience idea. Work shadowing provides an opportunity to watch somebody do the job to which you aspire. Employers won't be surprised by requests for work shadowing, and your local college or Job Centre may help you identify companies which are particularly keen on this and which could be approached.

It's a very useful way of determining whether this is something you want to do and of talking to a practitioner first hand about the advantages and disadvantages of working in the sector. It provides you with a chance to find out how they got involved, where they started out, and to make yourself known. It means that, if you wish to be a primary school teacher, you could approach a school – perhaps your children's old school – and ask if they would be willing to help you out.

Some sectors will expect you to have done some work experience

If you want to enter a very competitive area, such as media, then some relevant work experience will stand you in good stead. This may need to be done on a voluntary basis at first to get your foot in the door. The other very useful aspect of work experience is that you can talk to people who are working in the very sector which appeals to you. Once you have talked to them about the work they do, and the industry they are in, you can then ask them how they got there and who they think you should be talking to about getting a job.

Using government schemes

Some government-run training schemes may also offer a chance to get out in the workplace; it may be possible to put you with an employer in an area of interest that suits you. This works both ways: you each have the chance to learn more about the other and see if you are mutually suited! Schemes such as Work Trials may be running in your area. If you see a job advertised, you can apply with a letter explaining that you are eligible for a Work Trial. This means you are giving an employer an opportunity to see that you can do the job well. Work Trials may run for up to 15 working days. Hopefully, you will be offered the job at the end of these. Check with your Job Centre for details. From the employer's point of view, watching somebody on work experience means that they come to know them far better than they would just by interviewing. They can see how you fit in with the rest of the team, too.

Similarly, many training organisations also offer work experience placements as part of the package you receive.

Make the most of work experience.

Help out wherever you can; join in any activities that are going on of a social nature. Don't be worried about asking lots of questions – people would be concerned if you didn't. And remember, you won't be asked to do anything you're not capable of.

Knowing what makes a business tick

Business or commercial awareness is an increasingly necessary tool today. Take any two businesses which spring to mind – one should be a national outfit, the other a local one. Try to find out as much as you can in answer to the following questions:

◆ What are their strengths and weaknesses?
◆ What pressures are they under?
◆ Who decides what products they should market and sell?
◆ What threats do they face? What opportunities have they to expand?
◆ What do they do that is most effective?
◆ What could they do better?
◆ What happens if there is increasing legislation about the way they recruit staff?
◆ What impact is the euro having? How well prepared for it are they?
◆ What problems do they face?
◆ What tensions and power struggles might there be internally?
◆ Where do they get their information from about their customers and the economy?

Read what you can in newspaper business pages and indeed any articles relevant to your career sector of interest to find out what is going on. Talk to people at work – what do they think is happening to their organisation? To the business world? A questioning approach like this will help to build up your business awareness.

Try it now	◆ Ask people who have been in the workplace for a while how things are changing and how they are coping with those changes.
	◆ Find out what is on offer for you as a returner at your local college and at your LSC or Job Centre – you may be surprised.
	◆ If any of these things are suitable, apply for them. Failing that, talk to an adviser who knows your district well and can advise you as to the best route forward.

Summary

The world of work continues to change rapidly and you will need to show employers you have kept in touch with what is going on – and that you are willing to learn. Don't be daunted by this but view it as a challenge:

◆ There are an enormous number of opportunities for returners to work to catch up with the workplace.

◆ There is a very wide range of courses in all aspects of the workplace, from IT to presentation skills.

*Voluntary work
shows you're
enthusiastic and
motivated –
qualities
employers like!*

CHAPTER 11

Improving Your Skills Through Voluntary Work

'But I already *do* a huge amount of voluntary work', I hear you wail, or are you muttering 'Voluntary work – there's no point in doing something for nothing.' This chapter is going to show you how to direct your voluntary efforts into forming an integral part of your career planning.

Defining voluntary work

Anything you do without payment can be considered voluntary work. You might do it for a charity, a school, your next door neighbour, the old people's centre in the next street or delivering newsletters for the church. Over 20 million people take part in a voluntary activity each week.

> Voluntary work can be valuable in your search for a job, because it shows you have motivation and initiative.

Voluntary work can be an invaluable stepping stone to finding the right job.

Case study: Susannah becomes a teaching assistant _____

I'd had a short break from my sales job, and was looking for something to do to fill my time. The headteacher at my son's school heard and asked if I'd like to go in and help the kids with behavioural difficulties for a month, just listening to them read, that sort of thing. I did and enjoyed it – it was very rewarding, but I went back to sales. Three years later, the same headteacher rang. She wanted to take somebody on who would be a teaching assistant in the same unit – the staff had been impressed with my efforts the first time round and would I be interested in the post? I've been there two years now.

Voluntary work will increase your network of contacts. It will boost your confidence and your self-esteem, as your efforts will be appreciated. It will give you a chance to get back into the routine and discipline of work, perhaps working to achieve targets, while coping with emergencies and disasters at home. You may be able to get a reference, too. Try to relate the skills you've learned in your voluntary efforts to the job you want. You may need to target voluntary work particularly to give yourself a chance to develop relevant skills in a relevant environment.

How voluntary can work help you

Some people do voluntary work 'to do their bit', 'to help out', 'to give a bit back to the community'. This is particularly the case with the effort put into local charities, whether it is fund raising, selling goods in a shop, doing a flag day, counselling people in distress or helping with a jumble sale. Such volunteers probably have no idea that these efforts will increase their chances of getting a job.

Think more laterally than that. You might do voluntary work:

◆ to get insight into a job and the sorts of activities you might be doing day to day. You might shadow somebody, that is follow them as they go through a 'typical' day;

◆ to get at least the basic skill elements of a job under your belt;

◆ to prove that you're interested in the line of work you want to enter – this is always useful;

◆ to show that you have the ability to relate to the sort of people you would be working with, such as the elderly, children, or people with disabilities;

◆ to expand your skills base into areas where you want to work, such as counselling, advising, informing, promoting, selling, befriending, conserving, driving, fund-raising and recruiting.

You might even be able to pick up some units towards a National Vocational Qualification if you have the support of your 'employer', thereby enhancing your prospects in the job market.

Thus as a result of your voluntary work, your CV might include something like this:

2000–1 Receptionist at Stateside Hostel two afternoons a week

◆ assisted on reception at the hostel and made visitors feel welcome; explained the role of the hostel and answered queries as they arose; kept diaries for three social workers
◆ enjoyed working in a team and with a wide range of customers: the role frequently demanded patience, firmness, tact and an ability to calm down aggressive people.

The employer thus knows that, once you have been shown how his office systems work, you can function straightaway because you know how to welcome people, you enjoy teamwork and you have organising skills (keeping the diary).

When applying for a job as an assistant manager in a retail store, Angela wrote:

2001 Worked in School shop selling second hand uniforms

◆ ran shop with two women one afternoon a week
◆ responsible for handling money (cash, cheque and credit card transactions)
◆ promoted shop within the School at a wide variety of functions
◆ frequently worked rapidly under pressure
◆ maintained shop records; shop made a profit of [say how much], an increase of 14 per cent on previous year
◆ assisted in the production of an annual report to the PTA

Again, you will see that this shows a variety of skills – all gained through voluntary efforts. What's more, Angela wanted to gain more qualifications and, when she visited her local college, she discovered she could get credit for much of the work she had done voluntarily towards a National Vocational Qualification in Customer Services and Business Administration. All she had to do was to provide the evidence.

All this might have been incidental – the women doing this work may not have thought about their career plans when they started volunteering.

If you had a particular job in mind, you might be able to approach an employer and ask for some work experience to gain an insight into that job or at least contact somebody in a related field.

Case study: Dawn, now a teaching assistant _____

I wanted to work as a teaching assistant, but I hadn't got a clue how to start. Then a friend who is a teacher told me how badly some of the children needed someone just to sit and listen to them read for extra time each day, to improve their reading skills and build their confidence. I volunteered to help her, because I saw it as the ideal way to develop my skills and prove my interest. The next time a teaching assistant job came up, I applied and got it. The stint I'd done voluntarily certainly paid off – we talked about it a lot in the interview and I'm sure it showed I really was interested and knew what I was letting myself in for. For me, I proved to myself that was what I really wanted to do.

Choosing your voluntary work

Opportunities for voluntary work are fantastic and varied – you should be able to find something which relates to your interests and the skills you want to use. But how do you find it? Contact the National Centre for Volunteering by visiting their web-site, which shows the organisations that need help and which covers a range of areas such as sport, animal welfare, arts and heritage, conservation and the environment, young people and healthcare.

You could also 'deposit' some time with TimeBank, an organisation which matches the skills you want to use or develop, to charities in your area which need your help. Major employers such as Tesco and Boots are strong supporters of TimeBank and encourage their staff to participate, believing that it makes for better skilled, happier staff, and provides a selling point in their recruiting drives.

Finally, don't forget places like your local library notice board and local hospitals, *Yellow Pages* and charity shops. Also newspapers – the *Guardian* and *Evening Standard* run adverts with details of volunteering vacancies on Wednesday and Monday respectively.

The following organisations and activities are just a few examples of what you will find:

Blue Cross	Oxfam
Barnados	hospice shops
local zoos	NSPCC
environmental bodies	League of Friends of your local
Sense	hospital
visiting elderly people at	Mind
home	local churches
residential homes	political parties
local schools	local arts centre
committee work	hospital radio stations
campaign work	fund raising
advising people	counselling
entertaining others	writing publicity material
home checker	organising an event
helping children with	conservation work
reading problems	helping an employer with a
Sunday schools	project
selling Christmas cards	taking pet into homes
interviewing people	or hospitals

All these activities give you the opportunity to develop your skills and boost your confidence!

Choose your sector with care

Go for something that interests you, that you care about and really want to contribute to. You will find your efforts far more enjoyable and do a far better job! You may also find that, having gained experience in one sector, you might be able to find work in it.

Think about what you want to do in it

Case study: Pam, Oxfam volunteer

When I went into Oxfam, I was asked to fill in a form and tick those sorts of tasks I wanted to do. I didn't mind really – I was happy to do anything, but I did try to think about what I wanted.

Don't just say 'anything'! This is your chance to develop skills you might really want to use in work and which could thus broaden your job prospects. Try to focus on what you might want to do in the future and head for those things which will increase your chances of getting employment in them.

Don't worry about not having the necessary skills. One Oxfam shop stuck a board outside on the pavement, short and to the point:

> **Till Operator required**
> Will train if necessary
> Enthusiasm a must

Looking to the future

When you start any sort of voluntary work, find out whether there are any training courses on offer, either given by the organisation itself or which you could pick up at your local college. If you can gain a qualification, so much the better – some charities may offer you the chance of a National Vocational Qualification (NVQ).

Consider what you can do to expand your range of skills as much as possible. This may mean moving around shops, taking on different responsibilities and volunteering for different things.

Where your voluntary efforts might lead

Do these organisations have any paid posts which might appeal to you? Voluntary organisations are themselves huge and they have become far more professional in the way they do things. You may find an opening for paid employment within the voluntary sector, not just in the clerical, administrative and secretarial line but in fund raising and publicity, or organising campaigns. Many of these will have their own management positions, which could give you an entry. Some charities have posts for a Volunteer Manager – the person who coordinates the volunteers to ensure that there is adequate cover, and that volunteers are trained and motivated.

Plot the skills you're using and developing

Keep a note of all the skills you use in the course of your voluntary work so that you can use this information to sell yourself to employers, on your CV or at interview. Describe what you have contributed to the overall effort and explain how your role fitted in with the rest of the group. Were you a leader? Or a supporter? Did you advise? What particular skills and qualities did you offer that enabled you to add value to the group's efforts?

Analyse the impact you have made

Find out what impact you make on people when you meet them the first time. This may help you correct any possible weaknesses in your interview technique. Do you greet people you've not met before with a smile and a warm, strong handshake, keeping eye contact at the same time?

And then consider what impact you've made on the activities you've taken part in. Ask someone what they think. What difference have you personally made to the team effort? What value have you added? What did you do that nobody else could or wanted to do?

Keep your CV up to date

You don't want your CV to be too long – but keep a rough draft and add in the activities you are doing which show responsibility and how you're contributing to the team effort.

Case study: Janet, a manager in the retail sector _____

I gave up work after I'd had my two children, because I wanted to stay at home and look after them. It wasn't easy, but we managed on one pay cheque. I was always conscious, though, that one day they would leave home and so I kept in touch with the real world as far as I could by volunteering at my local Hospice shop. It kept my brain active, it helped me to learn a little about retail work, marketing, customer care, being assertive, the importance of training new staff and keeping others motivated. I also found that the employers I approached for work when I did go back were very interested in my experience working for the Hospice and it gave us something to talk about in interview. _____

Remember, employers like to see voluntary work on your CV

Examples of transferable skills you can extract from voluntary work which employers will like, include:

◆ team work – pulling together quickly with people you don't know to get something done;

◆ customer service skills – working with people from all different backgrounds to help them, meet their needs and exceed their expectations where possible;

◆ the flexibility to turn your hand to anything.

If the company you are applying to does a lot in the community itself, it is even more likely to be impressed by your efforts. Voluntary work shows motivation, enthusiasm and drive, and it builds self-confidence. You can also ask your voluntary organisation to write you a reference when applying for posts.

Try it now

◆ Identify the area of voluntary work you'd most like to help in. This may not necessarily be in your area – it could involve a two-week holiday abroad!

◆ Find out more information about what's on offer and the application process.

◆ Apply and give yourself a set number of things to learn and get skilled in over a given period of time.

◆ If you have done voluntary work before, see whether you can build on what you've done. If not, do a skills analysis as in Chapter 5 to work out what you've got from it.

Summary

Voluntary organisations offer an enormous number of opportunities to build your confidence, to increase your network and develop your skills, as do any activities you've undertaken unpaid and where you have given your time and energy freely.

◆ They have a huge number of employment opportunities so make sure you are kept abreast of these.

◆ Take advantage of any training you can get.

◆ Use them to develop and expand the skills you have to offer.

CHAPTER 12

Hunting for Opportunities

H aving decided the sort of work you want to do, you need to find out where the vacancies are so that you can apply. There are many avenues open to you; this chapter will cover some of them.

Looking at methods of job hunting

Talk to people you know who work in different sorts of companies, if you can, who are working at the sort of level you want to work at. Ask them:

◆ How did they first learn about the job they are now in?
◆ How recently did they get it?
◆ How did they approach their current employer?
◆ What advice would they have for you as someone going out into the workplace?
◆ What's the most bizarre method they ever heard of someone getting a job?

And then ask yourself:

◆ What have you learned about ways to get a job?
◆ How might their actions have changed your perceptions of job hunting?

The traditional methods of job hunting – looking in shop windows, checking the vacancy columns in the local papers – still remain. Go into any supermarket or bank and you may find vacancy cards pinned up on notice boards, or smart eye-catching posters with details of employment opportunities. One of the oldest methods of job hunting – word of mouth – is still one of the most powerful. 'It ain't what you know, but who', still goes a long way. And if you can think smart, you're more likely to land the sort of work you want.

Think carefully about how and where you are applying

◆ Where are the opportunities for work? (Notice I said work as opposed to paid employment); try not to limit your horizons to landing a permanent nine-to-five role. If you can be more flexible than that, you're more likely to land employment.

◆ How does the sector you wish to work in recruit? Word of mouth? Over the Internet? By advertising in the newspapers?

◆ How do the companies of the size you want to work in recruit? Small- and medium-sized companies are more likely to use a 'middle man' to take some of the effort out of the recruiting process; large companies will have large HR departments who oversee the whole thing.

◆ Use your network – remember that recruiting is an expensive business and employers want to reduce the cost *and* risk of taking on complete unknowns.

◆ What sort of methods of recruiting do you feel comfortable with?

For example, an employer may place an advert with a recruitment agency who puts the details on its web-site. If you are very happy using the Internet – for example, you do your weekly shop by this method – then you may be happy to go through the application process over the Net, registering your details, emailing your CV. If you prefer the human touch, then you may prefer to go into an agency on the street to investiage opportunities.

Advantages of using the Internet:

◆ It has a global reach so your search isn't restricted to local jobs. An employer on one side of the globe can recruit somebody with the skills they want, to work for them on the other, all via the Internet, perhaps with a telephone interview or video conference.

◆ Because of its global nature, the Net can be particularly useful if your partner's firm is relocating you.

◆ Recruitment can be speeded up dramatically.

◆ You can do it from home!

And the disadvantages:

◆ You need to check how often the web page is updated, or else you could be looking at very old information.

◆ Go with well known sites for security's sake if you are going to give personal details over the Net.

◆ It lacks the personal touch.

> Small firms don't have the resources for a personnel department; they are more likely to use word of mouth, local advertising or even a recruitment agency.

But do be wary of advertisements for homeworkers, of anybody promising to make you rich after you've signed up (and paid money) for a scheme stuffing envelopes or something similar. Never give any money to such schemes – you are unlikely to get it back.

If you are doing a college course, check with the careers office and the course tutors to see if any employers have approached them with vacancies, or can suggest people who are recruiting.

Use your network

Networking is one of the most effective ways to get the job you want. One third of people acquire their job through networking, as opposed to applying to advertised posts. It may simply involve meeting people for a drink or going the full hog and joining a professional or trade body and attending local meetings to get your name known. Build up your network of contacts and when you are ready to hunt for a job – or even a short-term contract – bring it into play.

◆ Talk to everybody you know, especially if they work, and let them know that you're looking for a job. Be specific about what you want. If you're vague, people won't be able to help you.

◆ Raise your profile and get seen. This may be at local events or areas where people working in the sector are known to socialise and meet.

◆ Remember that networking is a two-way process – be sure to see if there is anything you can do to help those you're talking to.

♦ Keep a mental note of things which your contact does, preferably in her personal life. Perhaps she's mentioned she has children, or plays a particular sport. Show you remember these details next time you meet her.

♦ Keep in touch without being pushy. Always write thank-you notes for any advice you've received.

♦ If you are able to, offer your services to cover people who are on holiday, even at the basic level. Once you get yourself known in a company and prove your worth, it is more likely to want to keep you.

Remember, people known to the company – or somebody in it – are less of a risk than the complete unknown. Some companies pay staff a bonus if they recommend a person for a post and that individual is ultimately recruited.

So let your intentions be known and ask:

♦ Do you know of anyone who would be interested in seeing my CV, or who is recruiting at the moment?

♦ What would your advice be to me?

♦ Which companies are expanding in this area?

♦ Is there anything I can do to help you or your company?

Making use of the local press

Many people see the paper as their main – if not their only – source of information on the jobs available to them. Don't forget that most papers will have the facility for you to surf their job pages on the Internet and ask for more information.

There are advantages in responding to an advertisement in the paper:

♦ you know the vacancy exits;

♦ you'll usually be given the name and title of the person to contact without doing any detective work;

♦ you don't have to look very far – buying the local paper may just involve a short trip to the newsagents;

♦ you'll get an idea of the range of vacancies and employers in your area.

But there are also disadvantages:

♦ you would be one of hundreds applying for one post

(everyone has seen it);
- ◆ the vacancy may have gone by the time the paper goes to press – somebody found out about it earlier;
- ◆ you have to read between the lines to get to grips with what the employer wants.

Employers want people with the right sort of:
- ◆ attitude;
- ◆ skills;
- ◆ 'fit' into the team, so that everyone will get on – the workplace is too demanding to have any oddballs in a team;
- ◆ qualifications, where appropriate.

They have to draw up advertisements that will bring them the sort of people they want to interview – and you must learn to read advertisements in such a way that you can work out what employers are looking for and whether you match their requirements.

Reading job advertisements

The following examples are included to show you the sort of things you need to look out for.

Mr Willing is General Manager of Let's Go Holidays in Middletown and wants to recruit a number of staff. You will see that there are some similarities between the three advertisements and some absolute necessities in each case.

WANTED
Person to help out in office
9:00 – 5:00
Must be cheerful, presentable and willing to do anything!
Apply, Mr Willing, Let's Go Holidays

Mr Willing wants someone who will turn up, be cheerful and willing to muck in with anything required – someone who won't turn their nose up at making the tea, and doing those routine tasks which can be dull. You need to show him that you're the sort of person who will happily do anything that is thrown at you – you're a team-spirited person.

He also has to recruit sales staff, because Head Office want to expand the presence of Let's Go Holidays in his town. So he places another advertisement:

WANTED
Sales People
Must have good communication skills, be able to work under pressure and be able to meet targets, also computer literate.
Experience in the travel industry an advantage.
Apply, Mr Willing, Let's Go Holidays

This advertisement demands people with specific skills, i.e. those who can:

◆ communicate effectively;
◆ work fast under pressure without losing their cool;
◆ meet targets set by Head Office and relayed to Mr Willing whose job it is to make sure that his sales staff all know what their targets are and can meet them;
◆ use information technology.

He would *prefer* to recruit sales personnel who have worked in the travel industry before (they will be able to achieve full efficiency more quickly) but he's not excluding anyone who hasn't.

Mr Willing also decides to take on a part-time Training Officer to ensure that his staff are getting the right sort of training they need in order to give them the best chance of meeting their targets. So he places one more advertisement:

WANTED
Part-Time Training Officer
Must have excellent communication skills, be experienced in providing training courses to meet the demands of an expanding business and *must* have experience of working in the travel industry.
Apply, Mr Willing, Let's Go Holidays

Mr Willing is still asking for communication skills (trainers must be able to work with a wide variety of people) but he is also expecting a trainer who can think about and meet the needs of an expanding business and produce tailor-made courses to help his people meet their targets. He *definitely* wants someone who was worked in the travel industry and would exclude anyone who didn't have it (unless they could win him over).

Although advertising has a part to play in recruiting, 70 per cent of jobs are not filled through advertising.

Using local recruitment agencies

A recruitment agency will try to fill a position for an employer. Many small and medium-sized companies may involve a recruitment agency in the search for suitable staff, partly because the agency will already have a pool of people on their books who may be suited to the position available, but also because recruitment agencies should know all about employment laws and will help them avoid the many legal pitfalls now involved in recruitment. For many companies, it is faster and less risky to enlist the help of a recruitment agency than to handle the entire recruitment process themselves.

Some recruitment agencies may specialise in a given area, such as:

◆ hotel and catering
◆ accountancy
◆ the media
◆ commerce/business
◆ working with children or the elderly
◆ nannies
◆ teaching
◆ legal work
◆ nursing

whereas others will cover all sorts of careers.

If you choose to log on to an agency web-site, it's worth noticing that if you register, some sites will alert you by sending you an email every time a vacancy of the sort you're looking for comes in. You can trail the site to find out what opportunities are available, double-clicking on those which may be relevant to you and finding out in an instant what the salary is, chief responsibilities are, and a bit about the company generally.

Companies like Reed and Manpower cover a wide section of careers from the hospitality industry to teaching; others focus on one sector of work.

Signing up with a recruitment agency

Call first to see if you need to make an appointment and take your CV with you when you go for your first interview. You will need to dress as if you were going for a job interview – the agency needs to know that you will represent them well; and you should know what you want to do – don't expect the agency to tell you what sort of job you ought to be looking for. Be honest and listen to any advice they give you about the way in which you market yourself. Take advantage of training they offer – it may be free.

Sign up with an agency that is a member of REC, the recruitment agencies' professional body. You know you're in a safe pair of hands then.

There are certain things you will need to bear in mind:
◆ Don't pay the agency anything – the employer who recruits you should be doing that.
◆ Don't sit at home waiting for them to ring you – keep in constant touch with your consultant and try to meet a couple of the others there if you can.
◆ Don't be pushed into the first job that comes your way; remember, it's your decision.
◆ Don't turn down something temporary if offered it just because it is temporary – you may be offered a full time job if you prove your worth.

Many agencies also offer temporary assignments, lasting for any length of time from a morning to a year. Temping is an excellent way to prove your worth, get experience, decide what you want to do, get the money coming in (you're usually paid weekly directly into your bank account) and to meet a future employer!

You make contact with the agency
↓
You meet with a consultant to discuss what you
have to offer and what sort of thing you are looking for
↓
The consultant looks for opportunities which might suit you
↓
An opportunity arises – the consultant calls you in to discuss
it or may tell you about it on the phone.
He/she should certainly brief you well about
the position and the company
↓
If you like the idea of the job, you attend for interview
with the employer – the consultant should have passed
all your details on to him or her
↓
If successful at the first interview, you may be offered the job,
or be asked back for a second interview
↓
Either you're offered the job – in which case you need
to decide whether to take it
↓
Or you're not – in which case,
the consultant keeps looking for you

Fig. 9. The job-hunting process through a recruitment agency.

How to sign up with an agency

The flow-chart in Figure 9 gives you an idea of the sort of
thing you might expect to happen. At every stage, your
consultant should give you advice, support and encouragement,
particularly after you have attended an interview.

Research the agencies in your local area

◆ Check the *Yellow Pages* for details, or the local papers.
◆ Try to find out what particular agencies are like through
talking with friends and family who may have used them.

♦ If you know of someone who has gone temping, talk to them about their life – this could include students at university or college, many of whom use agencies to get summer work.

♦ Find out what services they offer.

Creating a job by using your initiative

Expanding companies probably need more staff – so if you read in the press of a company which is planning to do just that, contact the employer to offer your services before they get a chance to advertise and are inundated with enthusiastic people. Send your CV with a covering letter directly to employers who might make use of your skills, interests and abilities. This could have one of three effects:

♦ you may be invited in for an interview;

♦ you may receive a letter stating that they have no vacancies at that time, but that they will keep your details on file – keep in touch by phone or letter at two- or three-monthly intervals if you're really keen on that company, reminding them of your skills and interest;

♦ you may be rejected.

This strategy is most effective when you have insider information that the company is going to have a need for a human resource, i.e. you have found out that they will need to take on staff to get a task done. Look carefully at any local news in the paper or think about the key times employers need to take people on. Often it may mean reacting very quickly to pieces of news you receive and getting in there first. The following headlines illustrate this:

♦ *Sorrell Electrics lays off 400 staff.* It creates opportunities for careers consultants who can come in to counsel those being made redundant.

♦ *Visitor numbers expected to rise as a result of new early-booking system.* This should promote action from tourist information officers, tour guides, and people organising outings for hotel staff.

♦ *Gardening Centre expands as gardening becomes increasingly popular hobby.* More opportunities for those interested in careers in horticulture retail.

Example

Vivienne Gray has taken advantage of an article which she read in her local paper recently concerning a garden centre which is expanding. She bites the bullet and writes to see if it might have need for her skills and interests, calling the main company number *first* to find out the full name and title of the person to write to. The letter she wrote is shown in Figure 10.

> **Show an employer what you can do for them.**

By her letter, Vivienne has demonstrated to a potential employer that she has:

◆ envisaged that the expanding centre might need extra staff; contacting the Personnel Manager immediately might enable her to avoid the lengthy selection procedure;

◆ thought about the skills which staff in a garden centre might need and mentioned them in her letter;

◆ demonstrated an interest in horticulture through mentioning her evening classes and reading and expressed a willingness to continue learning;

◆ mentioned her work in the local charity shop, proving she has background experience in retail;

◆ recognised that horticulture and pet care are two growth areas;

◆ proved that she has initiative by writing in;

◆ shown a keen interest in the centre and the job by writing in fairly promptly after the newspaper was published.

Mrs Green may not even have thought about starting to recruit staff, much less place an advert in the local press, so she may easily be delighted to hear from Vivienne and set up a meeting. On the other hand, the Personnel Manager of Greenhay Department Stores would probably not waste much time considering the sort of letter shown in Figure 11, which demonstrates that the writer has taken very little trouble over it. Compare Jill's letter with Vivienne's. Ask yourself:

◆ How much would the Personnel Manager have learned about each candidate?

◆ How much care had gone into each letter? Did Vivienne or Jill think more carefully about what she was writing?

321 Brown Lane
Littletown
Tel: 01234-56789

24 June 200X

Mrs Green
Personnel Manager
Gardening Made Light
123 Black Road
Littletown

Dear Mrs Green

I read in the *Evening Echo* on Thursday, 22 June, that your company is expanding your garden centre to take into account increased customer interest and demand. I wondered whether my skills and interest in this area might be of use to you?

I am seeking to return to the workplace after raising a family, and have strong communication skills. I can relate to people of all backgrounds while working under pressure. My voluntary efforts in our local charity shop have given me experience in customer service and ensuring that the shop is always tidy and pleasing to the eye.

I have always been interested in horticulture and pet care; I have attended local evening classes in plant management and read widely around the subject of pets from a practical point of view. I would be keen to continue training and learning about these subjects to improve my customer service skills and knowledge.

I am keen to return to part-time employment and would be available for interview at your convenience. I enclose my curriculum vitae for your information and can be contacted at home where my telephone number is 01234-56789.

I look forward to hearing from you.

Yours sincerely

Mrs Vivienne Gray

Fig. 10. A speculative letter in response to news of a company's expansion.

123 The Wall
Littletown

24 July 200X

Personnel Dept
Greenhay Department Stores
24 High Street
Littletown

Dear Sir/Madam

I am looking for a job in retail and wondered whether you might have any vacancies? I am enclosing a copy of my CV and would be happy to attend for interview. I look forward to hearing from you.

Yours faithfully

Mrs Jill Bloomer

Fig. 11. A letter which doesn't tell an employer a great deal.

◆ Who would you want to meet for interview and why?
◆ Which letter would have been most likely to get to the right person, rather than getting lost on a desk?

> **Think about the impact you hope to make and tailor your approach accordingly.**

Contacting employers cold

Another option when job hunting is to contact all employers who work in the career area you're interested in to find out whether they might have a vacancy.

Just drop in

You could always just stop by to see if a manager or someone in charge can talk to you about career opportunities, or at least give you an idea of what you need to do to get your foot in the door. Sometimes shops will advertise their career opportunities themselves in their windows. If you are going to drop in dress appropriately – not looking as if you've just finished the hoovering and dusting – take a copy of your CV with you and be flexible. If no one is available to talk to you at that moment, so be it – be prepared to go back: it shows you're keen.

Dropping in may be more appropriate for a smaller concern, but if you call at a large one the receptionist may call for someone from the Personnel Department who is likely to give you a brochure about the company and an application form to be filled in and returned. Smaller companies don't usually have brochures or application forms – they don't have the time or money for such things. That doesn't mean they don't offer great job opportunities.

Write to ask about a job

There is nothing to stop you writing to a company – locally or to a bigger branch – to express an interest in working for their firm. First, you might start by asking for any careers literature that might be available. At this point, try to show that you have done some research into the particular career or industry, and get hold of any company literature you can lay your hands on. Ask whether there will be any vacancies arising in the future. Don't forget to include your CV!

Call the company to ask about vacancies

Have a pen and paper in front of you, along with all your details, and write clearly on a piece of paper the person you're calling with their number. Speak clearly. Find out who is in charge of recruiting in the area you're interested in or who the manager for that department is.

Example

Eleanor Rushton is looking for a job in book sales. She gets through to a local book shop and to the manager there.

Eleanor: *Good morning, my name is Eleanor Rushton. I'm calling to ask about any vacancies you may have as a sales assistant.*

Mr Smith:	*I'm sorry, I'm not taking any staff on at the moment.*
Eleanor:	*Are you likely to be taking anyone on in the future, perhaps just before Christmas?*
Mr Smith:	*Yes, I usually take a couple of part-time staff on then.*
Eleanor:	*Could I send you my CV to look at? I've got experience of helping in a clothes shop, but I really wanted to work with books. I've just completed my English Literature A level and I read very widely.*
Mr Smith:	*Well, that sounds of interest. Can you drop your CV in to me and perhaps we could have a brief chat? Would you be looking for full- or part-time work?*
Eleanor:	*I'm happy to start with part-time work at the moment. I'd be as flexible as I can to fit in with the shop. Perhaps I could drop my CV in this afternoon – would that be convenient?*
Mr Smith:	*That'll be fine. I'll look forward to meeting you, then.*

Eleanor puts the phone down. She now has to get ready to take her CV, already prepared, to Mr Smith. She dresses appropriately, taking care over her appearance, notes down the reasons why she wants the job in books and reminds herself of the experience she has which might come in useful to Mr Smith. In particular, as Christmas is coming up, she notes that her children have given her useful experience, as a result of which she can advise parents and grandparents seeking to buy books for their children and grandchildren. She needs to think of all the things she can offer the company which somebody else can't.

So you see, you can turn a phone call to your advantage.

Try it now

◆ Identify the best routes to finding a job in the area you want to work in.
◆ Start actively looking for job opportunities.
◆ Begin to prepare your job-hunting tools – your CV and interview outfit.

Summary

There are many ways to find a job, even without reverting to the press, so:

- ◆ Make good use of all the facilities available to you locally and nationally to do your research.
- ◆ Care taken with letters will impress employers and will be more likely to make an impact.
- ◆ Keep notes of names, titles and companies in your careers file so that you can use them again.
- ◆ Don't be afraid to take the initiative and contact employers, rather than waiting for an advert to appear in the press.

CHAPTER 13

Producing Your CV

Two important things about a curriculum vitae (usually known simply as a CV) are to keep it short (two pages is enough) and relevant. Your objective is to get the employer to read it and grant you an interview.

In two pages you have not got room to give the employer your full life story. In any case, he or she wouldn't have the time or the inclination to read it. You have to be selective, so you need to choose the information that is more relevant, bearing in mind the sort of position you want and the kind of company that you are applying to.

Understanding the parts of a CV

A typical CV normally includes the following sections:
- personal details
- past work experience
- educational qualifications
- leisure activities and hobbies
- practical skills
- references

When putting your application together, aim to show what you can do and want to do. Essential key elements of a successful CV are that it is:
- accurate – check dates
- well laid out and easy to read, enabling the reader to make notes in the left and right margins
- honest about your qualifications and work-experience history, because most employers will check your background
- concise – use bullet points as opposd to paragraphs of prose
- relevant to what you want to do, with emphasis on the transferable and job-specific skills you will be using.

Mrs Josephine Ladel
Soupcon Cottage
Soup Lane
Littletown
(0001 000001)

1983–2001   Raised my family of three children. The boys are now 18, 16 and 14.

1980–1983   Joe Ellen & Co Ltd, Littletown
Secretary to Managing Director

1978–1980   Joe Ellen & Co Ltd, Littletown
Secretary to Personnel Manager

Educational Qualifications
1977–1978   Secretarial College

1972–1977   Littletown Girls School. 8 O Levels.

Hobbies and Interests
Member of the PTA

Tennis, badminton, going to the cinema on a Friday night

Fig. 12. A CV which says little about the applicant.

Writing a winning CV

Winning CVs show an employer what the applicant can do – they do not leave the employer guessing. How much does the CV shown in Figure 12 tell an employer?

The layout of this CV is not clear, nor does it tell the employer anything of interest. He or she may be able to guess what sorts of things Josephine did as a secretary – but would he or she have the time or energy to bother? On the other hand, the CV shown in Figure 13 sells the applicant.

Analysing a CV

Josephine Ladel is applying for a secretarial job within a leisure centre. Let's go through her CV in Figure 13 section by section.

Personal details

Josephine has put her personal details – name, address and phone number – in the centre of the page right at the top.

Mrs Josephine Ladel
Soupcon Cottage
Soup Lane
Littletown
(0001 000001)

Career Aspirations

Having raised my family, I wish to find employment within the leisure sector in a capacity where I can make effective use of my past secretarial experience while using those skills I have recently learned. An enthusiastic organiser, I enjoy working as a member of a team but can also work unsupervised to meet deadlines.

Work experience

1983–2001   Career Break: Raised my family of three children

- Developing skills in communicating, negotiating, organising and self-management; motivating and caring for others
- Responsible for financial aspects of the house, including budgeting house maintenance, holidays, insurance and utilities.

1980–1983   Joe Ellen & Co Ltd, Littletown, Publishing Company, 100 staff. Promoted to Secretary to Managing Director

- Responsible for six secretaries, including recruitment, induction and training, organising holiday and sick cover in cooperation with the Personnel Department
- Organised corporate events, including annual Christmas party for 250 people
- Responsible for sending out mail shot to prospective customers and recording up-take on database
- Organised Board Meetings, including preparation of documents, luncheon arrangements and minute taking.

1978–1980   Joe Ellen & Co Ltd, Littletown
Secretary to Personnel Manager

- Responsible for smooth running of interviews: arranged interviews with candidates, sent confirmation letters
- Verified qualifications with universities, colleges and schools
- Maintaining record system, audio typing (45 word per minute), photocopying, making refreshments.

Fig. 13. A CV which sells the applicant.

Educational Qualifications
1977–1978   Secretarial College

Acquired qualifications in audio typing (40 word per minute), shorthand (100 words per minute) and studied secretarial duties.

1972–1977   Littletown Girls School
Gained eight GCE O levels, including Maths, English and French.

Hobbies and interests
Parent Teacher Association, Littletown Secondary School Secretary (1999–2001); Committee Member and Secretary. Sent out agendas, took minutes, liaised with Chairman prior to meetings.

Tennis, member of local tennis club committee. Organised sponsored tennis tournament to raise £8,000 towards new clubhouse. 80 players took part over a long weekend. Played for the club in the second league.

Badminton, responsible for refreshment rota every Friday afternoon during the 2000–1 winter season. Organised members to serve teas, bake cakes, bring milk.

Films, particularly historical in nature.

Additional skills
- Computer literate: Windows 97, Word Perfect, Powerpoint, all acquired at evening class during the 1999–2000 academic year. Currently studying Excel through open learning.
- Conversational French acquired through adult education classes 1999–2001
- Clean driving licence
- First aid qualification acquired through St John Ambulance Brigade classes

Points of interest
- Marital Status: Married with three children
- Nationality: British
- Date of Birth: 9 June 1961

References
Available upon request

Fig. 13. continued.

They can be seen clearly here – in particular, the employer will have no difficult locating her telephone number.

Some people choose to put in two or three sentences about themselves and their career aspirations, such as:

> Motivated individual seeking a new career in financial services in an advisory capacity. Considerable experience assisting customers and identifying their needs, an interest in money matters and a belief that the financial services industry has much to offer have convinced me to seek an opportunity within it.

In our example, Josephine has given the employer an idea of the sort of job she is looking for and the sorts of qualities she will bring to it. This is a good example of a personal profile.

Past work experience

Josephine has described first the most recent thing she has done. An employer is more interested in what you've done recently as it is more directly relevant to them. Note that she has not made any apology for taking time out to raise a family. Rather, she has drawn attention to the things she has achieved and what she can offer. She has indicated to the employer the sort of companies she has worked for, and given an idea of the sort of level she worked at. If you have any gaps in your work history, explain them in your CV, because employers will certainly spot them and want to know what you've been doing in them. They are increasingly used to seeing people taking time out of the workplace for many reasons – travel, bringing up families, time out to fulfil a long-cherished dream – but the main thing is that you can explain your gap in a positive light.

Josephine has gone on to mention some of the work this has involved; but throughout the rest of her CV she has shown that she has taken on responsibility outside the home, for projects (fund raising for the tennis club), routine tasks (badminton refreshments) and learning (night classes).

For each job, you will need to be selective in deciding what to include or emphasise, depending on what the post you're applying for requires, or what you want to do for a company. If Josephine was applying for a post where looking after people was more critical, she might have placed more emphasis on her supervisory skills.

Educational qualifications

Put down those you've achieved in and after school. Demonstrate any recent learning you have done to prove you are able and willing to learn. If you can show that you have studied something which is relevant to the job you are applying for, so much the better. Most employers have not kept up to date with the changes in education, so describe what your qualification means. Make it simple – don't create work or a haze of wonder for them: '2000–2 National Vocational Qualification Level II, Information Technology' won't mean very much, but the same qualification expressed in the following manner will tell an employer instantly what you can do for his business:

2000–2   National Vocational Qualification Level II, Information Technology

- expert at keying into a computer
- experienced in using spreadsheets
- composed range of business correspondence
- currently learning to use Powerpoint

Put in any current classes you are studying. You can always put 'Results due June 2003' or 'to be completed in June 2003' after the name of the qualification you are studying:

Similarly, explain your skill in languages:

2001–2   French GCSE taken at Moorstown College of Further Education
Awaiting result. Able to converse in French and write simple business letters.

Try to give the employer an idea of the level you have acquired, rather than just saying 'French' or 'German'.

Josephine has chosen to list her computer skills under 'additional skills'. You will need to play with your CV and see where you think things like this fit best.

Spare time activities

These might include leisure interests and hobbies, voluntary efforts or points of interest which might be relevant, such as professional association memberships, clubs or societies. Anything that shows an employer you're a well-rounded person who likes to do things as opposed to slopping in front of the telly all day will be of interest. Try to show things that tell an employer you are a team player and adept at dealing with change and learning new skills.

Especially for you, the woman returner, the activities you've taken part in over the years while you raised your family can provide useful evidence of the skills you've developed and the qualities you can offer, and any responsibilities you've undertaken outside family life. Try to be specific about what you achieved:

◆ Fund-raiser for RSPCC: raised over £9,500 in one year by organising seven events in the community and through high-profile press coverage

says far more than:

◆ Member, RSPCC. In charge of fund-raising.

Be honest – don't put something down unless it really is a hobby. Your interviewer might be an expert on the subject!

Josephine has included things which relate to the job in hand – but then she really is keen on leisure activities. If she had put 'tennis, badminton and going to the cinema', and she did the first two only a couple of times a year, she would soon have been found out at interview.

Josephine also included the positions of responsibility she has held and what those involved. Her experience with the PTA was fairly recent and voluntarily given; she took the opportunity to refresh her skills in a way which might prove useful to the leisure centre's post.

Practical skills

Be very specific if you can, because your ability to add value to a team which may be lacking in such a skill might just hook you the job. You could mention:

- a clean driving licence; add any specific class of vehicle you can drive, e.g. minibus;
- first aid, e.g. with qualification;
- computer skills, e.g. familiar with Internet, email, word processing;
- languages abilities, e.g. conversational French, basic Spanish;
- numeracy skills;
- till operating skills;
- public speaking abilities, e.g. used to introducing guest speaker at monthly lunches for the Women's Institute.

Josephine has described exactly how she acquired her skills so that again she can be shown to have made an effort to go out and learn them.

Other points of interest

Put your date of birth, marital status and nationality under this section. If you leave off your date of birth, employers will wonder whether you are of the dinosaur era, so include it, but do so as 'date of birth' rather than 'age' – people are less likely to try to work out what that means in terms of actual years.

Referees

If you are going to give the names and addresses of (usually) two referees, you need to make sure that each one is happy to be one; and that they know what you are applying for so that they can make comments appropriately. Referees would normally consist of past employers, college tutors, voluntary work organisers – but not friends or relatives. An alternative is to put 'References available upon request' and leave it at that – but make sure you have two ready up your sleeve when the employer wants to know how to get hold of your referees.

Putting your CV in order

The order of the information in your CV depends on the individual it belongs to. School, college and university leavers usually put their educational achievements fairly high on a CV, over work experience, because they don't have much work history to put down. Adults are more likely to put their work experience first. You should put the most recent things first, because they are the most relevant to your application.

Ultimately, you will need to find a CV that you feel comfortable with. Try different formats and combinations until you are satisfied.

Examining different ways to write a CV

Josephine has written a chronological CV, but she could have written one which focused rather more on her skills (Figure 14).

Josephine has concentrated heavily on her skills by focusing on the main ones she has to offer which are relevant to this job and demonstrating them. However, although this sort of format should be the better self-marketing tool, the average employer is more familiar with the chronological CV which is often easier to follow.

Be descriptive

Josephine has used terminology throughout her CV that will appeal to an employer as she has chosen words that indicate she is active and can be entrusted with responsibility. Where possible, she has tried to show *what* she has achieved, or *how much* she raised or *how many* people she was in charge of. This all adds value and meaning to your CV. These are the words and phrases Josephine used:

- responsible for
- organised corporate events
- recording up-take on database
- organised Board Meetings
- responsible for smooth running
- verified with
- maintained record systems
- acquired qualifications
- liaised with
- organised
- raised £8,000
- played for
- organised members to
- collected money
- currently studying
- acquired through
- clean driving licence
- motivated others

Remember, your CV is your chief marketing tool so use words which will mean something to the employer – in other

Mrs Josephine Ladel
Soupcon Cottage
Soup Lane
Littletown
(0001 000001)

Career Aspirations

Having raised my family, I wish to find employment within the leisure sector in a capacity where I can make effective use of my past secretarial experience while using those skills I have recently learned. An enthusiastic organiser, I enjoy working as a member of a team but can also work unsupervised to meet deadlines.

Key Skills and Experience

Serving committees: organised Board Meetings and those of the PTA Committee. This involved: preparing and sending out agenda, organising location of meetings and refreshments, taking and writing up minutes, following up action points.

Taking responsibility: financial aspects of the family, including budgeting and liaising with insurance and utility companies; organised corporate events including annual Christmas party for 250 people at publishing company; liaised with applicants during time at personnel department.

Checking and maintaining records: verifying qualifications with universities as stated on applicants' forms and CVs.

Delivering results: my efforts at the publishing company ensured that the provision of secretarial services ran smoothly and applicants for posts within the company were dealt with efficiently. Raised £8,000 for tennis clubhouse through sponsored tennis weekend.

Managing self and others: raised a family while taking on responsibilities outside the house. Met deadlines. Took responsibility for my own learning by enlisting in adult education and open learning programmes.

Work experience

1983–2001	Career Break: Raised my family of three children
1980–1983	Joe Ellen & Co Ltd, Littletown, Publishing Company, 100 staff.
	Promoted to Secretary to Managing Director
1978–1980	Joe Ellen & Co Ltd, Littletown
	Secretary to Personnel Manager

Fig. 14. A skills-based CV.

Training, Education and Qualifications

1999–2001   Computer literacy classes: Windows 97, Word Perfect, Powerpoint
Currently studying Excel through open learning
Conversational French acquired through adult education classes

1977–1978   Secretarial College: Acquired qualifications in audio typing (40 word per minute) shorthand (100 words per minute), Secretarial Duties at Secretarial College

1972–1977   Littletown Girls School: Gained eight GCE O levels, including Maths, English and French

Hobbies and interests

Parent-Teacher Association, Littletown Secondary School Secretary (1999–2001); Committee member and Secretary.

Tennis, member of local tennis club committee. Played for the club in the second league.

Badminton, responsible for refreshment rota weekly during the 2000–1 winter season. Organised members to serve teas, bake cakes, bring milk. Collected money and paid into bank.

Films, particularly historical in nature.

Additional skills

Clean driving licence
First aid qualification acquired through St John Ambulance Brigade classes

Points of interest

Marital status: Married with three children
Nationality: British
Date of Birth: 9 June 1961

References

Available upon request

Fig. 14. continued.

words, relevant terms which denote *action*. You could use words such as:

- highly motivated
- proven record
- innovative
- ability
- negotiator
- control
- career
- strong work ethic
- reliable
- willing and able to learn
- productive
- dedicated
- pragmatic
- success/successful
- achiever
- development
- promoted
- positive
- mature
- loyal
- enthusiastic
- capable
- committed

Demonstrating you can keep up with change

Up-to-date knowledge doesn't last long. Since science and technology are moving forward so quickly, the knowledge acquired one moment tends to be out of date within a very short period of time. A classic here is computer science. You can buy the most up-to-date computer with the latest software and it will be old hat six months later.

The workplace is also changing at a frightening rate. These changes are caused by a number of factors, including local, national and international legislation, scientific and technological developments, greater customer expectations and a battle for customer loyalty and a global market.

But consider how you've coped with the many changes in your life, some of which might have included:

- becoming a mother;
- a relative coming to live with you or an important decision to be made about an elderly relative who can no longer care for him or herself;
- children growing up fast;
- husband or partner being made redundant or retiring;
- husband of many years leaving you or dying;
- getting married;
- getting divorced;

◆ getting a new job;
◆ changing town, country, region.

The life experiences that you have already been through demonstrate that you can adapt to changing circumstances and use tact and negotiating skills at the same time to keep everybody happy.

Getting feedback

It is very easy to make mistakes on a document, despite the wonders of the spellcheck button. So have someone you trust look at your draft CV for any errors or, just as important, gaps. Employers soon notice both.

It would also be helpful to have somebody run an eye over your CV with a view to making the most of any qualifications, skills or qualities you may have to offer. Take it to a Job Centre and ask an Employment Assistant to look through it, for example.

Try it now
◆ Produce a draft example of your CV.
◆ Now try to write it in another method described in this chapter.
◆ Think about which one works best for you.
◆ Show it to an adviser and ask what they think. Get someone to run an eye over it for spelling mistakes etc.

Summary

It is important to keep your CV relevant and keep it short – people do not have time to read waffle, so:

◆ You will normally have to re-write your CV for each new job – each job is different and your CV should be carefully targeted.
◆ Include any activities that show you've invested your time in something and developed skills.
◆ Remember that your CV is going to be your marketing tool and hopefully get you an interview – get it checked for errors.

CHAPTER 14

Writing to Apply

When you are approaching an employer with a view to acquiring a job with a company, you should try to catch his or her interest by demonstrating that you:

◆ care about the way in which you handle people;

◆ are willing and able to learn;

◆ can keep up with technology;

◆ work hard, are reliable and punctual;

◆ have relevant experience, skills and knowledge which can be put to use at once;

◆ welcome change and can adapt to it.

Apply for the position which is right for you and show an employer that you have skills and qualities that are relevant to the organisation.

Evaluating the job thoroughly

If the job was advertised, get more information. You may be asked to call or write in for an information pack and application form. Do as you're told, either way. Your letter could run something like the example in Figure 15. Include any job reference number which you saw in the advertisement; this will help the Personnel Section.

> **Focus on the things you *can* do and not the things you can't.**

Women focus too much on the things they *cannot* do instead of the things they can. Men focus on the things they can do.

On the advertisement tick all those things you can do. You should have very few areas that are not ticked if you have chosen the right job to apply for. Look carefully at those areas you can't do. Could you do them if you had some training?

1 Little Close
Newtown CH2 222
Tel: 01234-567890

18 October 200X

The Personnel Section
Newtown College of Further Education
PO Box 123
Newtown CH1 223

Dear Sir or Madam

Job Vacancy CG7

Further to your advertisement in the *Newtown Evening Echo* on Friday, 18 October, I would be very grateful if you would send me an information pack and application form.

I look forward to hearing from you.

Yours faithfully

Lisa Hope

Fig. 15. Writing off for information.

Well, then, apply. And stress your willingness to learn – even if it has to be in your own time. If you can point to recent learning you've done, this will demonstrate your desire to study and keep up to date.

Reminding yourself of your skills and qualities

Before you write in to an employer, make sure that you know exactly what you can offer them and why their company appeals. Make a checklist on a sheet of A4 paper, writing three or four points under each of the following key headings:

- My skills which would be relevant to this company are:
- My qualities are:
- The company interests me because:
- Research I have carried out on this company and key facts highlighted:
- Research I have carried out on the industry and key facts highlighted:
- I want this job because:

Keep this sheet with the copy of your application form and go through it again prior to your interview. Remember:

- The more research you do, the better prepared you will be in terms of your written application and the interview.
- Employers can see when an applicant has done thorough research and thought about their application; they see it as a sign of serious commitment and interest.
- Focus on what you can do and develop strategies for those aspects that you are not sure about.

Try to visit the company which is recruiting – their showrooms, perhaps, or branch – so that you can at least get an impression of what the place is like and see how happy and motivated the staff are. Find out what products and services they produce and about any promotions they are running. These are all things you can touch on to demonstrate your interest throughout the application process.

Some golden rules

Employers may use a number of different ways to fill a position. If they are advertising a post, they may ask you to write for a job description and application form or simply to send in a CV with a covering letter explaining why you would like to be considered for the post. They may be even more general than that, asking you to send your details (including salary).

> **Be brief. People haven't got time to read waffle.**

You may decide to write cold to an employer to see if they can use your skills and qualities. In this case, the most appropriate thing to do is to send a covering letter outlining your career aspirations with a CV outlining your experience and background to date.

Increase your chances from the start

Do as the advertisement asks. If you are asked to send a CV with a covering letter, do so. If the company wants you to complete their application form and send it back with a letter, but not a CV, do that. They may have very specific reasons why they want you to send one piece of paper but not another; follow their requests. Failure to do so may result in rejection. Essentially, companies are looking for ways in which they can compare applicants.

Entry qualifications

Employers and courses seeking people with certain qualifications for entry may set a standard for new recruits so that they know they have sufficient knowledge and skills to do their work competently. An employer may specify a set standard in English and Maths GCSEs (or the equivalent) so that they can be confident you'll have reached a certain standard. If you are considering a career for which you need to do a course first, find out whether the college has any age restrictions for that particular course.

Take pride over your application

There are some very simple rules which you should follow which will make sure your application at least gets a review.
Here are some do's and dont's:

Do	Don't
Check your spelling	Send in spelling errors
Use a clean piece of white A4	Use flowery notepaper, paper covered with coffee stains and creases

Check your grammar	Send in errors – if you can't be bothered to check your work for a job application, why should you be bothered for work?
Type or use a word processor if asked to do so	Hand-write CVs
Keep a copy of everything you send out to refresh your memory before the interview	Lose track of what applications are going out where. Keep them in a file and make a note of who's been sent what on a cover sheet
Be honest	Try to cover up gaps – employers will always ask you about these
Check the spelling and title of the person you are writing to	Start letters with Dear Sir/Madam – it only takes a phone call to check the name and title of whoever is in charge of recruitment
Make the whole thing readable and relevant	Send a photograph until you're asked to do so.

Some companies refuse to give out names and titles over the telephone. If this is the case, you have no alternative to put 'Dear Sir/Madam' unless you can get through to the Personnel or Human Resources Department and try to befriend someone on the phone. 'I wanted to send my CV in but I would like to address my covering letter to the head of your department by name, rather than Dear Sir/Madam' should be sufficient to get an answer.

> **Take pride in your attitude.**

Don't try to be witty or make out that you really will go mad if you don't get out of the house. And don't sound guilty about taking time out to stay at home to raise a family or run a home. Say you've done so with pride.

Completing the application form

There is as tendency – especially if you are applying for a similar job with a number of employers – to just put 'See attached CV' when asked to answer a question. Don't. Make the required effort. Employers use application forms as a means of comparing applicants for the position they are seeking to fill. Don't throw your chances away. Answer the question carefully. Think about why the employer has included it. What do they want to know? How does the question relate to the job you're going to be doing or the organisation itself?

> **Do answer each question – it's there for a reason.**

Don't leave anything out or any questions unanswered. If the post is very competitive, such gaps might well result in your form going into the bin. Some larger firms have computers to scan application forms for such gaps.

Always make a copy of the application form and practise filling it out first. This will give you a chance to see how your writing or typing fits into the space available and to think carefully about the questions asked.

Take a photocopy of the form after you've completed it and before you send it off so that you can run through your answers prior to interview.

You don't necessarily need to type the form – look for instructions on what to use and follow those. Remember that the employer may ask you to complete the form in black ink or on a typewriter – the reason for this is that blue ink does not photocopy well.

Using email to apply

Many people now send their CVs to prospective employers and recruitment agencies via email, rather than using the post. You can either attach your CV as a Word document or within the email itself, following a few lines outlining what you want to do, what you can do and why you can do it for the company you're applying to.

Using a fax machine

Sometimes, if you've heard about a vacancy that appeals and you're asked to send a copy of your CV, the fax machine can get your application there in record time. For a small employer who wants to fill a position as quickly as possible, this may make the difference. One travel agent put a note in a newspaper advertising a job on Wednesday. When the paper appeared at lunch time, one prospective candidate faxed her CV in straight away and then turned up at the office an hour later, after the boss had had a chance to look through it. She started work the following Monday. Now that's fast recruitment.

Complete the Further Information section

The Further Information section is where, in effect, a company says 'Tell us about yourself' or 'Is there anything else we should know about you which would be of interest to us?' They may even ask you to write an essay outlining why you want the job. Again, they may be seeking to compare your reasons with other applications but they may also want to see what your written communication skills are like, how persuasive you can be and how much research you've done into the company and job involved. Whatever form this section takes, it provides another opportunity for you to sell yourself, so don't waste it. Outline:

◆ your career aspirations, areas of interest for work and how much research you've done;
◆ the skills you have and the qualities you can offer;
◆ what has motivated you to return to work;
◆ the sort of work you are looking for and the sort of company you want to work for.

Practise this section several times. It can make a difference!

The covering letter

Don't race to do this. The covering letter is an important marketing tool. It sets the scene for your CV and introduces you to the employe. Figure 16 gives an example and explains what you need to include.

	(Put your address here)
	(The date)
Call the company to get the right name and title of the person to write to	Mrs Holmes (Title) (Company name and address)
	Dear Mrs Holmes
Give the job vacancy reference if there is one	Job Vacancy RG7
Explain why you are writing. Say how you heard about the vacancy	I am writing to apply for your vacancy for a Customer Service Agent, which was advertised in the *Evening Echo* on Friday, 18 November.
Explain why you are applying for the job	I am applying for this post because I would very much like to work in a customer service environment within the private sector.
And indicate any experience which might be relevant to the company	I have spent three years undertaking voluntary work at the local Oxfam shop, where I have gained experience in serving customers, handling cash, stock taking and answering queries about the organisation itself.
What can you offer?	I enjoy working with a wide variety of people and am patient and courteous, even when working under pressure. I particularly enjoy helping people and advising them on the products.
Explain when you could meet for interview	I enclose my curriculum vitae for your information and would be delighted to attend for an interview at any time, except for Wednesdays when I am currently committed to working at Oxfam. I can be contacted at my home telephone number.
Finish in a positive but pleasant manner	I look forward to hearing from you
	Yours sincerely
	(sign your name here)
	Sarah Spot

Fig. 16. Composing your covering letter.

Explain why you are writing and, if you are responding to a job vacancy that was advertised, give the title and explain where you saw the advertisement. Refer to it as an advertisement, not an advert.

If you are asked to respond to the advertisement with a handwritten letter, remember it could be because the company will analyse your writing to see what your personality is like and how you would fit their culture.

Each employer should have a different covering letter which explains why you have contacted their particular organisation.

Try it now	◆ Draft out a covering letter.
	◆ Work out what you would put to the request, 'Please provide us with any additional information that would help us in the application process'.

Summary

Always seek to sell yourself to an employer by showing him or her how the company will benefit from taking you on and what you can contribute to the job.

◆ Don't forget to explain why the employer appeals to you – massage their egos, a bit!

◆ If you can refer to research you've done, do so – it shows you're serious.

*Interviews are
two-way: they
find out about
you, you find
out about them*

CHAPTER 15

Handling Interviews

I f a company has asked you in for an interview, congratulate
yourself. You've made a good start! Interviews terrify the life
out of most people (including some interviewers), so this
chapter will help you prepare for your chance to sell yourself
in person and find out more about the job and company
you're interested in.

Make your preparation thorough

The company have invited you in because they want to find
out more about you and in particular what you might be able
to do for them and how you might fit in with the rest of the
team. You could have all the qualifications on earth, but if you
aren't a good 'fit', the team balance might be upset. This is also
your opportunity to find out more about the job, the company
and the people who work there – it's very much a two-way
process.

Organising the practicalities

You may be asked by letter or on the phone to attend for an
interview. Here's a checklist of things for you to find out and
keep a record of:

- ◆ Name of company
- ◆ Date of interview
- ◆ Time of interview
- ◆ Place (address)
- ◆ How I will get there
- ◆ Journey time
- ◆ Plans for dealing with any likely traffic problems, e.g. delays
  on the bus/train service, car parking
- ◆ Who I will be meeting
- ◆ Will I be able to have a look round the premises

- Will I have to do any exercises as in a presentation
- Any domestic arrangements I need to make
- Have I read through the papers I sent the company when I applied for the job so that I know what I wrote?

Think about your appearance

Make sure you dress the part, if you're not sure what the employees wear as a sort of 'uniform' see if you can watch some people leave one day and make a note of what they wear. If you're still unsure or can't do that, it's better to be safe than sorry and go for a conservative look. Some employers are more casual than others; some have a dressing down day on a Friday when staff can wear jeans, but for your interview you should dress up rather than down. Don't overdo the perfume, make-up or jewellery.

Preparation is the key.

Prepare your outfit

It sounds obvious and you've probably been telling your children to do this for years but:
- check that your interview outfit is clean and neatly pressed before the interview day itself;
- check that the car has sufficient petrol and that you know what the car parking is like in the area;
- get your hair done if you need to.

Know what the process may entail

Remember that employers assess prospective recruits using a number of methods – many consider it is too risky to stick to the traditional interview. Make sure you know what your time with the company will involve. Some methods may include:
- testing the specific skills you'd need to do a job – for example, you might be asked to teach a class for an hour
- a literacy, numeracy or non-verbal reasoning test
- a workplace-simulating test, seeing how you perform. This will show you what is important to the organisation, for

example, working well under pressure, how hungry you are,
accuracy, honesty

◆ a personality test to determine your strengths and
weaknesses

◆ hand-writing tests

◆ group exercises, to see how well you work in a team and
what sort of role you naturally veer towards

◆ presentation skills – asking you to prepare and give a
presentation for about five minutes.

You may also find that part of the selection procedure involves
your undertaking medical tests to prove you are healthy, where
you would have a medical with a company-approved GP;
background police checks, legally required if you are applying
for a post with children; and references acquired from referees.

Get some practice, if you can

Some local colleges, careers service companies, and Job Centres
may run short courses designed to help you boost your
interview skills. And there's no harm in sitting down with a
friend and having a run through answering questions. It will
help you to think on your feet! Don't get too practised,
however, otherwise if you're asked something that totally
surprises you, then you'll be thrown – possibly into a panic!

Understanding the interview process

Arrive early to allow for traffic problems and to give yourself
time to freshen up. If you are too early, go for a walk for ten
minutes. Treat everyone you meet with respect and in a friendly
manner; they may be your future colleagues and, as such, the
person interviewing you may ask them what they thought of
you after you've gone.

Make your initial greeting warm and friendly

You'll be invited into the interview, usually by one person who
will have been assigned the role of introducing you to anyone
else present. Smile, offer a strong handshake and make eye
contact when you're introduced to each person. You'll be

offered a seat; take it. Don't smoke even if you are told you can do so and if you are offered a drink, don't take anything alcoholic. Keep a clear head.

There will probably be some pleasant banter to give you a chance to settle down and relax a little. Remember that the interviewers will want to put you at ease as much as they can. They will achieve nothing by making you feel uneasy. They may ask you how your journey was, or make some comment about the weather. Don't be too negative, whatever your response.

Down to business

The interview may then take several forms, depending on how many interviewers there are. Often there will be someone from Personnel or Human Resources present to cover any formalities, together with the person who would be your immediate boss. They may start the serious bit by saying 'Now, let me tell you a bit about the company and what we're looking for'. You may find yourself trying to put in a couple of words over the next half hour!

They may kick off with, 'Well, Janice, tell us a bit about yourself'. Interviewers like this question. They are not looking for a reply like this:

> *'Well, I am 38 years old, and I've got brown hair and I'm five feet four. I've spent the last ten years raising my children and I like tennis and badminton. I've got four children and three dogs. My husband works in an electronics plant.'*

This candidate has not told the interviewer very much – he can see from meeting her what her appearance is like and she has told him nothing about her skills and qualities that would interest him. Something like this would be more appropriate:

> *'I've spent ten years raising my children and, now that they are older, I've decided to return to the workplace. I've taken a course in IT to update my skills and I'm looking for a position which will enable me to use my abilities to help people and advise them. I was treasurer for our PTA shop, so I'm used to*

handling money. A career as a financial adviser appeals very much – I'm keen to learn and develop my skills.'

This second answer shows the interviewer that she:
◆ has updated her skills in IT, recognising that IT has had a great impact on the workplace;
◆ has skills in helping people and advising them;
◆ has past experience in handling money and an interest in it;
◆ is willing to learn.

Using questions in the interview process

Many interviewers use the open question technique, designed to make you talk and answer their question with more than the words 'yes' or 'no'. 'Are you pleased with your results in your Access course?' only requires a yes or no answer from you, and doesn't demand any need to expand. 'Tell us how you felt about your Access results' is an open question, expecting you to respond in several sentences.

Some interviewers may used closed questions (those requiring just a yes or no answer) to shut up candidates who won't stop talking. Aim to answer questions clearly and with thought – but don't waffle for the sake of it. Be economical with your words.

Anticipating questions

If you were recruiting someone for a post, what would you want to ask them? Or if you were meeting someone who thought they had skills and knowledge which might be useful to your company, how would you find out more?

Here are some questions you might be asked. How would you answer them? Keep the job and company you're applying for in the back of your mind so that you can relate your answers to the position.
◆ What are your strengths and weaknesses?
◆ Why do you want to work for us? Why not our competitors?
◆ Why should we recruit you over somebody else?
◆ Tell us about yourself.
◆ What do you know about our company?

- Tell us about a problem you've had to solve. How did you approach it?
- Where do you see yourself in five years time?
- Give us an example of something you've done that you're particularly proud of.
- What appeals to you about this post?
- Tell us about your experience with ...
- Why are you coming back to work?

If you are asked what other jobs you are applying for right now, don't give them the impression that you're trying for as many jobs as possible. It will make recruiters think that you don't care about the sort of job – or employer – you have. Show you're serious about wanting to stick to the line of work you're applying for.

Interviewers may also ask about things you've done – recently and a long time ago, either in or out of work – so be prepared.

Employers are *not* supposed to ask you about the arrangements you have made for your children: some assume that, since you are applying for a job, you have already taken care of this. You could always approach the subject yourself, by explaining that you have a very good back-up system in the event of an emergency.

If you don't understand a question, or want more time to consider an answer, or simply don't know the answer, then say so. Don't waffle or try to bluff your way through. There are some other important 'don'ts' to remember, too.

- Don't say you're returning for the money even if it's true. Everybody needs money.
- Don't say you want the job because the hours are convenient.
- Don't smoke or drink alcohol, even if you are offered a cigarette or alcohol.
- Don't lie.
- Don't ask about pay early on – wait until the interviewer introduces it.
- Don't complain about your last boss and company or blame others for problems you've experienced.

Finally, your interview may be with a team of people. If this is the case, maintain eye contact with the person asking the question but glance at the rest of the team as you answer it. Make sure you connect with each individual.

Thinking up questions to ask

An interview is also your chance to find out more about the company. Having visited the site and perhaps even been shown around, and met some of the staff (at the very least, the person who welcomed you and let your interviewer know you were there), you will have had a chance to think about whether you really want to work in such an organisation. So think about what you want to get from the firm and a working environment. Refresh yourself on the work you did earlier in this book: what are you looking for in your future company? Think up some good questions to ask – but they should not centre on salary, holidays, perks etc. There will be time for those later. Here are some questions you might ask which demonstrate a thoughtful approach:

◆ Tell me about the management structure here.
◆ Can you describe the relationship between management and staff? Are ideas encouraged from the bottom up?
◆ What training is available to me?
◆ How does this company assess staff on their performance?
◆ Am I replacing someone or is this a new post?
◆ Tell me how you joined the company (to interviewer). What do you like about it?
◆ Where does the company see itself being in the next five years?
◆ Who will I be reporting to?
◆ What is the make up of staff working for the organisation?
◆ What is the next step (i.e. where do we go from here)?

Try to find out how many women work there who, like yourself, have returned to the workplace. If there are quite a few, that's a bonus. Perhaps the company is particularly sympathetic to women returners.

Things to look out for

It is difficult when you're arriving for an interview and the butterflies are hard at work in your stomach to think about the place you're walking into, but try to note the welcome you get, whether the receptionist knows who you are (gives an idea of how their internal communications work), what the decor is like, e.g. do the walls need a fresh coat of paint or are they smart and warm and welcoming?

Visit the ladies. Are they clean and well stocked with loo paper? Are there any extras such as hand cream, tissues? What sort of cups/mugs are coffee and tea served in? Chipped and dirty or pretty china? Does the coffee come out of a machine? Could you drink the stuff from Monday to Friday? Do you have to pay for it?

Do the staff look happy, interested and awake? Are phones leapt on every time they ring or left for a minute or two? Is the boss's office substantially superior to where everyone else is working? If so, this should give you an idea of what the boss thinks of the rest of the staff and how important they are.

Making an impact

Smile, however nervous you're feeling. Make eye contact with everybody you meet, looking them straight in the eye. If you are being interviewed by more than one person, remember to look at each person in turn so that you make contact with them all.

Listen well

If you're listening to something that's being said, nod to show you're listening, make agreeing noises, such as 'Yes, I see' at regular intervals. Don't interrupt the interviewer in the middle of a sentence, however often he or she may do the same to you!

Try to keep your hand gestures to a minimum: don't fidget or put your hands in your pockets. Avoid slouching, sit upright, leaning forward slightly.

Don't get chummy

Apart from the first few moments when the interviewer may be seeking to put you at your ease, try not to talk about your children, pets, the difficulty of parking in the area or what you did last Friday night, however friendly he or she appears to be. Keep to the point – the job, the company and what you can do for them.

Show you've done your research

At any opportunity you can, show that you've done some research. Even if you've just walked into the sales area and had a good look around, that shows you've taken an interest and done *something*. If you've noticed an article on the company in the paper, seek out an opportunity to say so. Your serious and interested approach will impress. Comment on their web-site to show you've visited it.

Don't leave them wondering why they should recruit you!

Listen to this familiar comment made by the Personnel Manager of a supermarket chain after an interview with an applicant, Janice:

Case study: Janice, attending an interview _____
She talked a lot about what our company could do for her, putting lots of emphasis on our training programmes and career progression routes. She made the right noises there. But I'm still left wondering: *what she can do for us?* _____

Following up

Take a deep breath! It's over. When you have left the building and got away, take a deep breath and congratulate yourself! You've done it! You've got through it. Now is a good time to think about what you handled well and which questions you found difficult. Which bit had you found the most nerve-racking? How did you handle the difficult interviewers and how would you do things differently next time? If you went for the job through a recruitment agency, you should have an opportunity to discuss how the interview went. At the same time, the employer will let the agency know how you got on.

What happens next

You may be asked back for a second interview, perhaps to meet more people who will be working with you, or even to do a presentation or some games to find out more about your abilities in a team.

You may have been offered the job on the spot. Don't accept it at once. Tell them that you've enjoyed meeting them and that you'll get back to them. Ask them to put their details in writing. Talk salary, terms and conditions.

You may receive a letter rejecting you. It's natural to feel disappointed. Some companies will elaborate on why you failed, whereas others won't because it is their policy not to explain why you didn't get the job. You could call to see whether they will give you feedback on your interview performance and how you might improve it next time. It could be that there was simply someone else out there who was better suited to the company and post.

Try it now

◆ Think about what you can offer the company and what you would want from it.

◆ 'Tell us about yourself'. What would you say?

Summary

Preparation is the key to success in any interview – the more thought you put into it, the more you will get out of it.

◆ Be prepared to go back a second time.

◆ Relax and don't get too tense!

◆ Take in as much of the environment as you can when you attend for an interview so that you can assess whether you'll be happy working there.

◆ After you have left, reflect on how you handled it all to see if there is anything you need to learn before the next occasion.

*Look after
yourself as you
get down to
work and into
your new
lifestyle*

CHAPTER 16

Coping With Those Initial Weeks

G reat! You've been offered a job, either by letter, or on the
phone, or even at the interview. So what should you do
now?

Accepting the job offer

It is often a good idea to think the offer over for a couple of
days. This may seem like a strange thing to do but if the person
who had offered you the job was in the same position as you,
they'd probably want a couple of days before finally saying 'yes'
as well. Don't let them pressurise you into accepting.

> Take a couple of days to check that the company and the
> job really are the right ones for you.

Ask yourself some searching questions

How did you feel about walking into the organisation? Did it
have a genuinely welcoming feel to it? Did you feel as though
you would fit in well there and look forward to going to work?
Are there chances of promotion? What training and support
will you get? Did you get the feeling that the company will be
sympathetic to family requirements?

Deciding between two job offers

You may be in the fortunate position of having to decide
between two offers. There's always some hedging to be done
while you try to decide which job to take. A gut feeling will tell
you which one to go for. Write down the pros and cons of
each company and see which one matches your needs more
closely than the other. And don't forget the importance of the
cultural fit – if you felt much happier in one than the other,

then perhaps your choice has been made for you. Remember, you can always talk through your situation with a careers adviser.

Signing a contract of employment

You'll have to sign a contract of employment. Read it carefully, keep a copy for yourself, sign it and return it with a covering letter (see Figure 17).

White Cottage
Fishing Lane
Fireburn ABC DFE
Tel: 0111-111111

24 November 200X

Mrs Dewhurst
Personnel Manager
Lexco Building Society
2 High Street
Fireburn ABC DF1

Dear Mrs Dewhurst

Thank you for very much for your letter offering me the post of administrative officer with your company.

I have now read the contract of employment and am delighted to return it to you, duly signed as requested. Please let me know if you need any further information.

May I say how much I am looking to joining your company on 2 January 200X.

Yours sincerely

Carla Longing

Fig. 17. An example of a covering letter accepting a job.

Other documents

You may have to sign a Confidentiality Agreement, which means that you promise to keep everything you see and hear at the company relating to business to yourself. You may be asked for a medical certificate saying that you are fully fit and have a good health record: the company may specify a particular doctor or it may be possible for you to go to your usual GP. You'll also need to make sure that the company has details of the bank account into which your salary or wage is to be paid, unless it is in cash.

Settling in

Prepare for your first day as if you were getting ready for the children's first day at a new school. Get your clothes ready in advance; make sure you know how you're going to get to work, allowing for hitches with transport. Many companies ask new members of staff to arrive slightly later than everyone else on the first day, so that the staff can all get settled in and answer any urgent messages before turning to make the newcomer feel welcome. In any case, try to arrive a few minutes earlier than the time you're asked to and, if you're driving, make sure you know what you'll do with the car when you get there. If you don't feel like eating breakfast on your first day, take in some fruit or something similar to eat later.

What should I wear?

If you didn't take in what everybody wore when you went for interview, go and watch people leave one day after work to get an idea of the dress code. Don't go for anything too short, tight, sexy or clingy. You may look terrific, but it's not right for work. Don't wear jeans and leggings unless they are obviously appropriate.

If you want to go higher, observe your superiors in the company and wear something similar to them. If you dress like a secretary, you're likely to remain one. Look the part and you'll feel the part.

Arriving

As you're shown to your position, you imagine that all eyes are upon you as the newcomer. Most people remember what it's like to be new, and they'll do what they can to help you settle in. Asking questions is a good way to get to know people. You'll be full of enthusiasm and eager to be there; they may be in that work mode which means they don't show any overriding enthusiasm for being at work, but if they won the lottery tomorrow, they would probably still go in for the companionship, the buzz and the gossip. In the meantime, they just get on with it.

Give the time needed to form good working relationships. Take part in anything you can – going to the pub after work for a drink, or joining them for lunch.

Basic practicalities

You should be told where things like the ladies are, where the coffee is and whether you have to pay for it, where you can hang your coat up, and other essentials.

You should also be given thorough instruction in health and safety, although this is something that many firms overlook. In particular, you should be told what the fire alarm sounds like, where your nearest exit is and what to do if that's blocked, and where to assemble once the alarm has gone off and you're outside. In practice, too many organisations don't bother. Make sure you find out. If you are working in a job where you are responsible for others, it is particularly important that you receive these sorts of instructions.

Getting down to work

Some companies may start off giving you a fairly easy run so that you get into the work slowly and they don't give you too much to get used to at once. If you are not busy, show team spirit by asking those who are whether there is anything you can do for them. One day, you will probably appreciate a similar offer of help. Find out if the company has any specific rules about the way in which it produces correspondence and what happens about mail collection. Don't take on too much at once.

> Try to excel at everything you do to show yourself and your new employer you're capable of more.

In a larger company, where you may find you are one of several new recruits starting on the same day, the company may run a short course designed to introduce you to the organisation and its ways of doing things. However confident everybody looks on the induction course, they are probably suffering from first day nerves too. If you're experiencing lots of butterflies, then smile, show an interest in others and people will never know you're nervous!

You may receive training on any IT systems the organisation has, such as email, word processing and any databases it uses. Don't worry if you feel you're picking up things more slowly than other people are. IT trainers are used to working at all sorts of speeds.

You may also get a tour around the company to meet everybody so that they know who you are. People won't expect you to remember all their names as a result. An organised company will have sent a memo or email around to tell everyone that you're starting and to explain what your role is: 'Barbara Courtness will be starting on Monday, 11 October, as an Administrator in the Loans Department. Please make her welcome.' Some companies leave the tour around the building until you've settled down a little – especially if the organisation is a large one.

Let your partner know how to contact you

Just in case of an emergency of course. Don't spend your first morning making personal calls to tell all your friends and family how you're getting on, even if half the staff seem to be organising their social lives from the office. Some organisations monitor the calls their staff make.

Using information technology

Don't worry about asking lots of questions about the computing systems if you're stuck. It's always better to ask if you don't know. Your colleagues will be pleased to help – people who have learnt to master the computer are usually very happy to pass their new-found knowledge on to others. If your colleagues sitting nearby can't help, contact the IT department or company expert, if there is one. Someone, somewhere will know the answer to your question. Just ask!

Don't hesitate to ask for help.

Take a break from your computer

The Health and Safety at Work Act provides for this but in reality it simply doesn't work. Constant headaches, repetitive strain injury and back problems arise because employees don't take breaks from their computer – then their bosses wonder why they have to go off sick. It's easy to forget to take a break, and it's impossible to do so when you're in the middle of something urgent (which invariably gets forgotten by those who wanted it because they've gone off to lunch).

Dealing with colleagues

Many firms recruit young people after their A levels or degrees on management development programmes. They may be young enough to be your son or daughter and they may be your supervisor or boss. Show a serious approach to the work, offer to stay to finish something or help others out when you can, show you're prepared to study for courses in your spare time – and they'll soon realise that you are a serious worker. Then, when something happens and you have to ask somebody else to take over, they'll remember all the those times you've helped other colleagues out. Remember that they are learning too.

Problem colleagues

If someone is upsetting you, try not to show it in public: count to ten. Sound in control. Look this person straight in the eye. Remain cool and calm if you can. Some people are often sharp with others because of the pressure they deem themselves to be under.

If the person upsetting you is your superior, and you feel their actions are unjustified – perhaps they keep on criticising you, bullying you or giving you far too much to do – take notes of the things they are doing that are making your life a misery. Approach the problem in a constructive way. Ask for a meeting and go through things your supervisor does well to boost his or her confidence, but then give some examples – a couple will do – of what they do that you don't enjoy. They may not realise that they're upsetting you. If the problem persists, take it higher – but make sure you've got lots of evidence to back you up, so that you can give examples of your supervisor's poor behaviour.

Dealing with sexual harassment

If a colleague or client is making you feel extremely uncomfortable by his constant sexual innuendoes or comments, record every incident which upsets you. Note the day, time, what happened and whether anybody else was there. Within your company, report the matter to your supervisor or the Personnel Department. You can, between you, then confront the guilty party with his behaviour. Outside work, you can turn to bodies such as the Equal Opportunities Commission. The alternative is to make a joke of his behaviour and scold him as if he were one of your children. But never, ever be alone with him in the office when everybody else has gone.

Email and the Internet have their own dangers

Many employees use email for personal reasons, such as sending messages to your friends – 'How was your weekend? Drink tonight to catch up?' and sending jokes. Some email message lists resemble the advice column in a magazine. Some companies access their staff's email messages to see how many of them are personal. Make sure you know and abide by the company's policy on the personal use of email. Some will fire staff if they find any porn, jokes or personal messages.

On the Internet, staff may have – and use – access to porn. If you supervise staff, their use of the email and Internet may be something you'll have to monitor. Talk to other managers to see how they handle it. Many companies have a policy of instant dismissal if email and Internet are used inappropriately.

186 Returning to Work

Enjoying the office party

Go, enjoy, relax and have a good time. Even if the drink is free, don't get wildly drunk. Your behaviour may be noted.

Contributing to company success

You know how much you appreciate it if somebody offers to go that extra mile for you. You sit up and think, 'I'm going to use that company again'. Business is very much about showing an interest in your client's affairs and showing a willingness to help. It's about building a relationship with your customers and helping them through times when they have difficulties and times when everything is going well.

This is why it is so important to recruit people who are professional and really take pride in their work and who are passionate about doing it well and helping others. Even if you are 'just' a checkout operator, your attitude and the way in which you greet your customers and offer to help them pack, makes an impact.

> People judge a company very much on the attitude and performance of its front-line staff.

If the member of staff who assisted you was useless, the company may well lose you as a customer. Every single person in a company has a responsibility for its growth and reputation to attract new customers and retain existing ones.

Meeting deadlines

Excelling in business isn't just about the smile and showing the caring face to a customer. It's also very much about delivering what you say you will, well within the deadline. If you call a company for information and that doesn't arrive within a day or so, you start to feel that the company is letting you down. they don't really care whether or not you get the brochure. That organisation has failed to deliver. And if they can't deliver a brochure, what will the rest of their service be like?

Getting the job done and anticipating a customer's needs are an integral part of excellent service. As you are served by staff over the next few weeks in any capacity, think about the service you're being given. Rank the standard. How could a member of staff demonstrate even further that they care about the standard of service they are giving you?

Think back to the last time you were served by someone who clearly didn't care what you thought of their service. What impression did this leave you of their company? Did you go back, given that you have a choice of companies to choose from? Or did you choose to take your business elsewhere? Knowing how you reacted, what can you do at work which will make a difference to the way in which customers view your organisation?

Performance reviews and appraisals

Companies use all sorts of methods to reach their goals. They may undertake staff performance reviews to see whether staff have met their targets and where they need to improve or need help with training. They may pay staff by results and/or reward a team for its performance or the whole company for the year's results.

Performance reviews and appraisals, together with team briefings, will help you focus on what your job involves and how it is changing, how it is contributing to the organisation and team, and what sorts of skills and competencies you will need to acquire to cope with future changes. A review will help you identify what you need to do to carry out your job well and how you might do it even more effectively than you are at present. It is less likely to be undertaken in a small company or family-run firm than it is the large one. Prepare well for your review – make a note of your achievements and areas in which you feel you need more help. Think about where you see your career going.

Continuing to train

Keep learning! The workplace is constantly changing, partly due to new developments in technology but also to political, economic and legislative developments. For instance, any new European directives from Brussels will have an implication on the way in which business is done, for example with regard to health and safety regulations.

There are many ways to train now. Most training programmes will be organised and planned specifically to meet the needs of the company. Some larger companies offer in-house training, either buying in trainers or producing their own. In a smaller company, you'll probably have to take on more responsibility for your own training programme, although your employer may help with the expenses and/or study leave.

Companies may use a variety of training methods, including:

◆ on the job training – learning by doing
◆ secondment
◆ evening courses
◆ in-house training, done by training officers employed by the firm
◆ correspondence courses
◆ national vocational qualifications
◆ day release courses, i.e. one day a week at college, the remaining four days at work
◆ role play
◆ video and feedback
◆ study for academic qualifications
◆ giving presentations
◆ work shadowing
◆ mentoring.

Many employers have facilities for learning with dedicated-learning PC facilities or an Intranet, or buying in existing products or developing their own in-house. And many companies, large and small, will develop partnerships with local colleges and universities to acquire training courses to meet their needs.

Keep track at home of any training courses you do – they are all something to tell your next employer about when you apply for a job! Ask your supervisor how you can develop your strengths and tackle your weaknesses.

> Every time you do something new, you are building your skills and confidence.

Be prepared to train in your own free time

If you are working for a company and you want to develop your ability in a particular area, be prepared to study at college to further your portfolio of skills in your own free time. You can always take your newly-gained skills elsewhere.

Continuing professional development

In many professions, continuing professional development is expected of all staff. This is particularly true in any area where there are going to be huge changes, such as architecture, surveying, banking and financial services, medicine and dentistry. Customers expect those serving them to be up to date in their knowledge and skills and so the staff must keep training.

Many professions will also expect you to take up membership of their association and/or to study for examinations the professional body has set. This is in order to maintain the standards set by that body so that the public may have confidence in its members. An example: if you were to call out a new plumber, you'd want that tradesman or woman to be qualified, experienced and to know what they are doing, wouldn't you? A professional qualification and membership of the professional body signals that the tradesperson has met the standards required.

Try it now
- Find out who the various people are who can help you in the company. Make sure you know how to get hold of them.
- Develop a plan to show your commitment to the team, so that if your home situation becomes difficult at any time you can be sure your company will be happy to help you because they don't want to lose you.

Summary

Make sure you're not too hard on yourself during the first few weeks – expect to be more tired than usual as you get used to your new office.
- Don't be afraid to ask for help – either at work or at home.
- Let people know if there is going to be a problem.
- Keep in touch with your family's needs and feelings – but be assertive about what you need too.
- Don't feel guilty. You owe this move to yourself. One day, you may be the main breadwinner for the family – if you're not already.

| CHAPTER 17

Managing Your New Lifestyle

Work is tiring! There's lots to learn, not just about the actual job itself but also about the way the organisation works. Particularly in the first few weeks, you need to look after yourself as you adapt to your new lifestyle.

Looking after yourself

If you are finding things stressful:

◆ reduce the amount of caffeine, alcohol and cigarettes you consume;
◆ take a Vitamin B supplement;
◆ treat yourself to a beauty treatment once a week;
◆ go to bed incredibly early one night of the week with a good book – let the family know that you want a quiet evening;
◆ get plenty of exercise;
◆ field calls at home with an answer phone.

Business versus family life

Don't be surprised if, once you start, the business ignores your family life, whatever promises were made to you at interview.
In fact, if you *expect* the business to ignore family life, you'll be in for less of a shock. Provide back-up plans for your family so that, if you absolutely have to work late or go in on a Saturday, you're covered.

Prioritise what is important to you

Prioritise what is important to you after you've finished work, and keep checking to see if your priorities are changing. Once you've started work, you may find you haven't got the time you once had to see friends. There may also be people you don't want to stay in touch with whom you'd happily have an excuse to see less of.

Buying yourself time

There are a number of ways in which you can make your life more efficient.

Get a wall planner

These are available from any stationers. Put yours on the wall where the family can see it and use it, and start planning. There are various coloured stickers you can use to denote an activity. For example, any dates which are school or college related – such as the Christmas concert, parents' evenings – can go up in one colour, birthdays can go in another. Dental, doctor's, vet's and garage (MOT) appointments in another. Put as many things as you can – and encourage the family to do the same – so that you don't have to keep trying to remember things in your head. Similarly, display a list of telephone numbers that are important so that you don't have to keep looking them up.

Shopping versus working

Know the opening hours of the local shops both near your home and your workplace so that you – or your partner – can pick up the odd bits you've forgotten. Keep a supply of emergency meals for the freezer and a list of takeaway/delivery services next to your wall planner. Use the Internet or the telephone, for your weekly supermarket shopping – you order what you want and they deliver. Not all supermarkets offer this sort of service, so check to see if yours does. And buy in bulk.

Get a mobile phone

They're really useful – for telling the office you're on the way and stuck in traffic or the train has been cancelled again; for calling the kids from the train to let them know you're on the way home; to order that takeaway dinner so that it will be ready for you to collect as you pass. And very useful if the car breaks down.

Coping with emergencies

If you cannot go to work because you are ill, speak to your immediate superior in person to let him or her know. Bosses are suspicious of messages passed through a friend in the firm. Sound really sorry that you can't be there. Many organisations are open-plan so if you are suffering from flu/a cold/stomach bug, it may well be better to stay away until you really are well again, as bugs fly around open-plan air-conditioned offices speedily. Stay at home, and don't go out unless you really have to. It could bring an unwelcome result if another member of staff saw you out and about when you were supposed to be home ill.

Dealing with family illness

No matter how well you prepare for the eventuality, the day will come when you get that phone call at work or at home in the evening which means that your working hours are going to be disrupted because of a family crisis. What can you do?

1   Make sure it really *is* an emergency and not a relative just trying to persuade you that work really can do without you. Could you pop in early in the morning to see how they are on your way to work and leave work slightly earlier than usual to check on them again at the end of the day?

2   Find out whether anybody from your support network could help you out, even if it's just for an hour so that you can pop into the office and get some work to take home with you. You could still take calls at home which are work related and there may be other projects you can continue to work on there.

If you need to be absent – speak to your boss. If this is not possible because he or she is in a meeting, the next best thing is to leave a message with a member of staff explaining that you won't be in and asking your boss to call you at home so that you can explain your absence. Try to pick up some work if you can – or put in lengthier hours when you return to make up. It's annoying but women are still the ones who have to sacrifice their working day when something like this happens.

Talk to your partner to see if he can help – you could take it in turns to cover the emergency.

Dealing with long-term sickness

A member of your family falls ills and it's up to you to look after them. Increasingly, organisations are trying to be more sympathetic when people's dependants are having problems, but you need to do what you can to keep working. Going into the office may well provide the break you really need if you're at home a lot looking after a dependant. The companionship, the work and the gossip will take your mind off things.

Find out whether there are any community services you can turn to, either private or public, to help you look after elderly relatives. Even if you have to pay for someone to pop in, at least it gives you the break you badly need.

A teleworker situation might be possible, where you work at home linked up to the office, going in for a morning a week or for the occasional meeting to keep in touch.

See if you can change your role slightly. You could reduce the hours you're working – perhaps you can find a friend who will be willing to job share, for example. You might be able to alter your role slightly so that you can delegate some duties to other members of staff while taking on others that are more easily performed at home. Talk to other members of the team to see how they would be affected by this idea.

Let the company know early on if there's a problem

If you know that you're going to have a problem at home, then don't keep the problem in the dark. Your concentration at work may suffer anyway; you may make silly mistakes through worry. Put in the extra effort while you can and let your supervisor know how things are going. If it's not good, try to come up with solutions as to how you might be able to continue working while looking after your relative. One solution might be to offer to cover for colleagues when they are on holiday – it will give you the break you need and some much needed cash.

If the company fires you for being honest and looking after your family, they weren't worth working for from the start.

Changing relationships: family and friends

You may find that, owing to changes in your life and how you approach everything, you are suddenly moving away from family and friends. You are a new person, because you've gone out to the workplace, you've made new friends and developed new interests – and they may well have stayed the same.

> **Make time for your family and friends – they are more important than housework.**

Try to think of things you can do with your friends that will minimise the amount of work you all have to do and maximise the enjoyment and fun you'll have with them. Why not agree to meet up at a pub rather than have someone slave over a hot stove? Or go on a picnic or just out for a walk? There's no substitute for fresh air, exercise and good food to keep the stress levels down.

Spend time with your partner

Build time into the week to be alone together. Do things that are fun and make you laugh. You may find that you want to take on more responsibility at work, which could mean longer working hours and so less time for you to deal with household chores; or you may end up bringing work home. Keep the lines of communication open. And remember that your partner may be having thoughts, successes and difficulties with his own career, so be a good listener for him and encourage him.

Set goals for the year together

Set your own individual goals, but aim too for something you can do *together*, so that you can achieve some goals jointly. Take the example of a couple whose kids had left home. They decided that every month they would do something together they had never done before. So far, they've gone hot air ballooning, had a romantic weekend away, tried a new restaurant and taken part in a day's adult education class focusing on local history. The extra money Angela is earning goes in part to pay for these monthly treats. The result? They're having a truly wonderful and very happy time.

Some ideas for something new could include:

◆ a major holiday to a more exotic destination;
◆ putting money into an extra savings account for retirement;
◆ learning a new language together;
◆ buying a new car;
◆ buying a dinghy;
◆ taking up a new hobby you can enjoy together;
◆ renewing your wedding vows with another honeymoon.

If something doesn't seem to be possible, ask yourselves why
and then work out a way to overcome the problem together.

Making time for you

Don't be surprised if, when you get home from work, you need
half an hour or so to unwind and just be quiet. If you allow
yourself to be run ragged, you'll end up exhausted, stressed,
then ill and possibly depressed. Take time out to do whatever
you enjoy doing. Give yourself full permission to slump in
sloppy clothes in front of the TV with a packet of nibbles and
a glass of wine. Buy that bar of chocolate and munch it
without feeling guilty. Have a face pack as you soak in the bath.
If you find this sort of thing difficult to fit into the day,
schedule an appointment with yourself.

Remaining employed

The days of the job for life are over (parenthood excepted).
The best you can aim for is to be employed doing something,
but not necessarily with the same employer and certainly not
doing the same job. How can you stay employed?

Stay aware

If you are working in a large organisation, it is easy to be blind
to all the changes that are taking place. Watch what is
happening to your company: is your department under threat,
are staff reductions likely? What would you do if you were
made redundant? What can you do to boost the reputation of
your department, both as an individual and as a team?

Maintain a high profile

Make sure you *want* to move on and that you've got everything under control at work and at home. Otherwise your standard of work and your relationships both with those you love and your fellow colleagues might start to decline.

Get about a bit. Talk to people you don't know to find out who they are and what they do. Join committees, take part in social events. Copy memos you've written with a great new idea to managers higher up. Put forward well thought out solutions to problems. Come up with creative ideas, which give the company smarter new ways to do things. Expand your skills in the company's time and your own. Tell your supervisor you want to move up and you're keen to take on more responsibility.

Keep an up-to-date copy of your CV ready at home. You may find an opportunity suddenly comes your way and somebody says, 'send me a copy of your CV, will you?' A client may put in a good word for you to someone he knows in a similar business and you could be on your way. Be prepared for such opportunities. Of course, you may turn them down – but you may be thrilled that such an opening has come your way.

All this probably seems daunting at first. As your confidence grows, and your natural common sense asserts itself, you'll find yourself in a good position to do all these things.

> Be alert to opportunities – inside your company *and* outside it.

Take control of your life

Organisations themselves cannot control many of the things happening today, so they certainly can't control your career with any degree of stability. You have to take control of it yourself; the responsibility is yours. This is what has made career planning so interesting – and challenging.

Any job will, if a company is moving forward and changing, alter itself without the aid of a job description. Those who are not willing to learn new skills and take on new projects are those likely to be forced out.

You'll only be disappointed if you expect a job to be
permanent, i.e. for the rest of your working life, because:

◆ *Your job* should be changing anyway, reflecting changes that
   the company is going through (and it must, if it is to
   survive).

◆ *You* will change in terms of what you want after you've been
   working for a while.

You may find that you want to move on to another job within
the company or even move companies; you might need to
move to a different part of the country or abroad because of
your partner's job. You might decide to become self-employed.
You never know.

Don't expect others to stay around

One of the things you may well notice is that people join and
leave a company very quickly nowadays – especially those in
the 20–35 age bracket. They are very much looking after their
own career development and moving on if they can find a new
challenge elsewhere. You may join a firm and have a new boss
only to find several months later that she/he has gone and
somebody else takes their place.

Expecting your job to change

In the old days, personnel officers wrote out carefully drafted
job descriptions which were rigidly adhered to (aided by union
pressure). Everyone knew exactly what they had to do and
when and there was a very distinct hierarchy with a formal
atmosphere. This was okay, because the world wasn't changing
at the speed it is now.

Today, although job descriptions exist, outlining the specific
duties and responsibilities of the post-holder, employees have
to be willing to do more than the job description says. In a fast
changing world, job descriptions are too rigid. Consequently,
companies want to take on people who can welcome and cope
positively with change. Those who dislike and fear it are going
to suffer.

> The company changes from day to day – so why shouldn't your job?

If you're running your own business, join any local or national business organisations so that you can network with others and raise your profile (and that of your business) in the community.

Strengthening your position

Of course, some people are quite happy as they are; they don't want the extra responsibility. That's fine too, but what sort of position would you be in if you're made redundant?

Expanding your CV

Aim to re-write your CV every year, even if you remain in the same level of job, by adding to it new responsibilities, extra skills, and/or possibly new qualifications. If you cannot alter your CV, it means that you haven't progressed your development. Offer to take on new projects to develop your skills and your confidence – the more you do, the more you will probably feel like doing.

Securing your future

In the light of today's insecure employment climate, you need to do all you can to secure your future – and that of your partner, if you have one. Try doing regular 'SWOT' analyses, either on your own or together.

S   Identify the Strengths you have

W Know your Weaknesses

O   Identify Opportunities out there for you to strengthen your position, financially, as a couple, or as an individual.

T   Threats – know what is out there to threaten your happiness or security. Then take steps to make sure you're protected.

Analysing your current position in this way will help you prepare better for the future. You will be able to identify problems before they become too great to deal with.

◆   Study for any qualifications which will strengthen your position in the job market as a whole.

◆ Get financial advice to make sure you're safe for the future. Put money aside into a pension fund. Get a financial health check every year or so. Know what your money is doing for you. Find out where you can make savings.

◆ Get health checks every year or two years. Have a Well Woman and a Well Man check. You do an MOT on the car. Why not on you?

◆ Analyse your time. Is there anything you're both spending time on that you'd rather not, or people you're having to put up with that you'd rather not?

Try it now	◆ Work out your goals for the following year.
	◆ Do a SWOT analysis.

Summary

Expect everything to keep changing – not least yourself. Keep your partner aware of those changes – don't produce any surprises.

◆ Keep learning and expanding your skills and knowledge base if you want to remain employed.

◆ Expect your job to change, even if you still have the same title. A job which doesn't, isn't healthy.

CHAPTER 18

How Far Do You Want to Go?

I t's difficult to know what will happen to you when you get to work. What started out as a gentle job to bring in some extra cash may suddenly unleash a passion to go further, either up the management route, or specialising in a niche area, or starting your own business. You may simply just want to remain *in work*.

Keep your progress in view

Whatever you're thinking of doing next, research your options carefully so that you know which one is best for you, your family circumstances and your career plans.

Progressing with your company

Susan spent eighteen months working as an administrator. She was stunned when one day, her manager asked if she would like to be considered for promotion. He explained that her new role would involve supervising ten or so staff, including taking responsibility for their induction and career development, and monitoring the department's workload. 'I was so pleased,' Susan explained, 'because I had worked really hard and it just seemed as if all my efforts were being rewarded. I'm now studying for my NVQ Level in supervisory management and enjoying new challenges. I learn something new every day!'

Asking for more responsibility

If you want to move on and up, ask your boss if there's anything you can do to ease their load! He or she won't give you anything well over your head to do. Ask if you could join a working group or committee that might benefit from your skills, perhaps an inter-departmental group, so that you get to know others outside your own area. Take as much responsibility as you can handle. You could be surprised where your career might end up. And don't wait for it to come to you. *Go out there and ask for it.*

Leaving the company

The idea that somebody should now spend 40 years with the same company has been blown out of the water by modern circumstances, although many employers recruit more mature people because they are more likely to be loyal and *not* move on. And you may well find that you're happy to stay where you are.

> **The most important person to be loyal to is you.**

On the other hand, your supervisor and personnel department may hold slightly different views of your future from yours. You may want to go in one particular direction which they might not be able to cater for, anyway. And let's face it, if a glass ceiling is preventing you from moving on higher up the company, you can leave and take your skills and abilities to somewhere where they will be valued. It's your company's loss – and your gain. Don't be held back by lack of opportunity or a company's unwillingness to meet your career aspirations.

Starting your own business

Case study: Miranda, Franchisee, Recruitment Agency _____
I'd been working for a recruitment agency for a year, interviewing people who came in through the door. I thought, I could do this for me. I started to look around for a franchise – I thought it would be safer, it was too much of a risk for me doing it all on my own. We've been set up for three years – it's going really well. I've never looked back. _____

> **What do you want out of work and life?**

Seeking more qualifications

Once you've put your toe in the water, you might discover you just want to dive right in and go for further qualifications, having had the chance to observe first-hand those whose career has progressed further than yours.

Case study: Sandra, Trainee Teacher _____

Whatever you started out thinking, it's important to stay open minded and to be prepared to move on. I spent a term helping a teacher in a classroom, became more and more fascinated by the work she was doing – and I thought, I could teach. I'm now doing a four-year full-time B.Ed. programme – I love it. But I never thought I'd be doing it when I first went back to work. _____

You don't have to study full time. Monica has chosen to do an Open University course in management, studying at home at night after work. She loves it – especially the residential course in the summer – because it gives her a new lease of life and a feeling that she is doing something for herself, 'after all these years!'.

Talk to your supervisor

Find a quiet time when you can discuss your career with your supervisor or boss. This may be during your performance review and appraisal, if you get one, when you can talk about the direction you want your career to go in. Then you can raise the subject of studying for further qualifications. If you work for a small company where you don't have an opportunity to sit down with a boss and talk about your goals, seize the right moment and talk to your boss about your wish to study. If your career goal is to do something completely different to what the company is expecting you to do, keep it quiet and go it alone.

What has your local college got to offer?

Go back to your local college. Find out whether they offer any relevant courses. If you want to progress up the career ladder within your own organisation, there may be certain qualifications that would help you do that, such as an Introduction to Management course or a National Vocational Qualification. Remind yourself that increasing numbers of people are studying on their own initiative at their own expense, out of working hours, to ensure that their career moves in the direction they want it to go and to increase their chances of remaining in work.

Would the company be willing to sponsor you?

Ask if and how the company might support you. They might offer study leave, money for books, or payment of fees etc. You never know until you ask!

Small companies may not have the resources to be as generous as large ones in terms of sponsoring your studies or giving you study leave. When you speak to your boss, show him or her how your efforts would help you do your job more effectively and help the company grow.

Career Development Loans

Career Development Loans enable you to study a vocational course which is relevant to a job – not necessarily your present job – over a one- or two-year period. See Useful Addresses for more information.

Moving on

At the beginning of this book, Figure 1 (page 2) showed what happens when people lose interest in their work. Dissatisfaction starts to creep in – boredom, frustration, the feeling that it's time for a change. If this happens to you:

> **Take action before your performance is affected.**

If there's no sign of a promotion in sight and you're hungry to move on and up, it might be time to look outside the company for your next move. At that stage, your network may be useful again.

If you move on to another firm, working out your notice period can be extraordinarily difficult, because you want to leave on a high note but you're already thinking about your new job so it's hard to be enthusiastic and concentrate on what you're doing. Remember you need a good reference – and you might go back to your old company in the future!

Reviewing your goals in life

Goals should be:

S Specific
M Measurable
A Achievable
R Realistic
T Time set (establish a time in which you must achieve them)

Don't push your goals out of reach.

While you can reach for the stars, if you keep falling well short of your goals it can be pretty self-defeating and disheartening. Set yourself *realistic* targets, which you think you can achieve; and then enjoy and learn from the journey to achieve them.

Review your goals with your partner and children

You may find the whole family working together more as a unit if you share your own individual goals and aspirations. You are in a better position to help each other, especially when the going gets rough. Put up a chart next to your wall planner and get everybody to put their goals on it, work related or otherwise. Every time somebody achieves one of their goals, celebrate and go wild. We celebrate too little in this life.

Review the way you spend your time

This is particularly important as your priorities and interests change. Six months or a year on, things that initially you were determined to keep a hold of yourself have lost that importance. Suddenly, it may not matter very much if the housework isn't done as often as you used to do, because it's more fun to be at work. Consequently, keep reviewing your activities and the time you spend doing them: you may decide it would be better to pay somebody else to do some tasks. At least you're creating a job for somebody else.

Stay in control

Don't let your job take over everything else if you don't want it to. This is not easy. It may mean leaving your present organisation and moving on to a more sympathetic one. Women are twice as likely as men to take time off for stress-related reasons.

> Remember – companies don't want to lose good employees to competitors: they need every good team player they can get.

Try it now
- Think about where you want to be in five years time, ten years...
- Ask your family the same question.
- Do something to celebrate all that you've achieved. Do it with family, friends and family, or just friends. But do it.

Summary

Think about where you see yourself going in two years' time. What do you want to achieve? At work? At home? In changes made to your lifestyle? Set yourself some goals.

- Discuss them with the rest of the family, especially your partner if you have one. Compare notes. How can you reconcile the bits which don't meet up?
- Look forward to the future and congratulate yourself. Celebrate your achievements. The rest is up to you and your aspirations.

Further Reading

Careers

Feel the Fear and Do it Anyway, Susan Jeffries (Arrow Books).
Great Answers to Tough Interview Questions, Martin-John Yate (Kogan Page).
Learning New Job Skills, Laurel Alexander (How To Books).
Occupations, published annually by COIC and available in libraries and
   bookshops.
Returning to Work: A Directory of Education and Training for Women (Longman).
Starting a Business From Home, Graham Jones (How To Books).
Successfully Going Freelance in a Week, Brian Holmes (Institute of Management,
   1998).
Surfing the Net, H. Nickell (How To Books).
The Times A–Z of Careers and Jobs, Sandhya Sharma (Kogan Page).
Writing a CV that Works, Paul McGee (How To Books).

Returning to education

*Higher Education and Disability: The Guide to Higher Education for People with
   Disabilities,* available from Skill (see Useful Addresses) for a fee.
The Mature Student's Guide to Higher Education, available from UCAS (see Useful
   Addresses) free of charge.
Student Money Matters, supported by UCAS, published by Trotman & Co.
University and College Entrance: The Official Guide (also known as the 'Big Book'),
   available from book shops or in your local library, published annually.
What Do Graduates Do?, published annually by AGCAS in association with UCAS
   and CSU.

Useful Addresses

Department for Education and Skills. Helpline: 0870 000 2288, www.des.gov.uk or visit the Adult Learners Gateway which has lots of information on courses at every level and on financing them.

Learning and Skills Council. Tel: 0870 900 6800, www.lsc.gov.uk

Job Centres, Employment Service. Check your *Yellow Pages* but also log on to www.employmentservice.gov.uk

New Deal. www.newdeal-gov.uk or visit your local Job Centre.

Women Returners' Network. Send SAE to WRN, 344–354 Gray's Inn Road, WC1X 8BP. Tel: 020 7468 2290.

Caring for others

Carers National Association. Freephone 0808 808 7777 from 10.00–12.00am and 2.00–4.00pm Monday to Friday.

Daycare Trust (for help finding and choosing good-quality childcare). Tel: 020 7840 3350, www.daycaretrust.org.uk

Kids' Clubs Network (for out-of-school clubs). Tel: 020 7512 2100, www.kidsclubs.com

www.dess.gov.uk/lifeevent/famchild (for information on caring for others).

Education

Association of British Correspondence Colleges, PO Box 17926, London SW19 3WB. Tel: 020 8544 9559. Will send out a brochure with information about courses and colleges available.

The Basic Skills Agency, 1–19 New Oxford Street, London WC1A 1NU. Tel: 020 7405 4017. Helpline: 0800 700987, www.basic-skills.co.uk

British Dyslexia Association, 98 London Road, Reading RG1 5AU. Tel: 0118 966 8271, www.bda.dyslexia.com

Career Development Loans. Tel: 0800 585 505 (8.00am–10.00pm Monday to Friday), www.lifelonglearning.org.uk has more details.

Educational Guidance Services for Adults. Free independent services which will help you find out more about courses in higher education. Contact your local careers services company for details of your local office.

Learning Direct. Free information and advice on learning opportunities and careers. Helpline: 0800 100 900, www.learndirect.co.uk

National Extension College, Michael Young Centre, Purbeck Road, Cambridge CB2 2HN. Tel: 01223 450200. Provides a range of correspondence courses

including GCSEs, A Levels, degrees and higher education, career and business
skills, counselling and guidance. Visit www.nec.ac.uk

National Institute of Adult Continuing Education, 21 De Montford Street,
Leicester LE1 7GE. Tel: 0116 255 1451. In Wales contact: Wales Committee,
NIACE/CIACE Cymru, Welsh Joint Education Committee, Education
Department, 245 Western Avenue, Cardiff CF5 2YX. Tel: 029 20 265000,
www.niace.org.uk

Open College of the Arts, Redbrook Business Park, Unit 1B, Wilthorpe Road,
Barnsley, S75 1JN. Tel: 01226 730495. Offers courses in creative arts such as art
and design, creative writing, drawing, garden design, history of art, music,
painting, photography, sculpture and textiles. Home study with back-up from
tutors in various educational institutions. Visit www.oca-uk.com

Open University, Central Enquiries, PO Box 200, Milton Keynes MK7 6AA. Tel:
01908 653231, www.open.ac.uk

UCAS, Rosehill, New Barn Lane, Cheltenham, Gloucestershire GL52 3LZ. Tel:
01242 227788, www.ucas.com. It has information for mature students,
including details on where to start, how to apply, what happens after you've
applied and financial advice.

WEA (Workers' Education Authority). For information about courses in your
area, call Freephone 0800 328 1060, www.wea.org.uk

www.hotcourses.com for lots of information about courses throughout the
country. If you want to acquire skills-based learning, it is particularly useful.

Job hunting

Skill, 4th Floor, Chapter House, 18–20 Crucifix Lane, London SE1 3JW. Tel: 020
7450 0620 (minicom); information service 0800 328 5050; minicom 0800 068
2422. Helps those with disabilities or learning difficulties. You can also visit
their web-site, www.skill.org.uk

Working for a Charity, 4 Bloomsbury Square, London WC1A 2RL. Tel: 020 7242
3606. Send an A4 SAE for information.

These web-sites may be useful:
www.charityconnections.co.uk
www.fish4.co.uk
www.jobs4publicsector.com
www.jobsite.co.uk
www.manpower.co.uk
www.reed.co.uk
www.stepstone.co.uk

For recruitment agencies, also check *Yellow Pages* under Recruitment and
Employment Agencies

Lone parents

Child Support Agency national enquiry line. Tel: 08457 133 133, www.dss.gov.uk/csa
Gingerbread. Tel: 020 7488 9300.
One Parent Families. Tel: 0800 0185 026, www.oneparentfamilies.org.uk
www.newdeal-gov.uk for information on the New Deal scheme for lone parents.

Running your own business

The British Franchise Association, Thames View, New Town Road, Henley-on-Thames, Oxfordshire RG7 1HG. Tel: 01491 578 049. Offers help and advice in evaluating franchise offers; information guide and franchise manual for a fee. Visit their web-site, www.british-franchise.org
Business Link. Tel: 0845 600 9006 (England), 08457 969 798 (Wales, Business Connect), or 0800 787878 (Scotland, Scottish Enterprise), www.businessadviceonline.org
Commission for Racial Equality, Headquarters, Elliot House, 10–12 Allington Street, London SW1E 5EH. Tel: 020 7828 7022.
Employer's Helpline. Tel: 08457 143 143. Can help with basic tax matters or national insurance enquiries. Also provides basic information on registering for VAT, statutory sick pay and maternity benefit.
Equal Opportunities Commission, Arndale House, Arndale Centre, Manchester M4 3EQ. Tel: 08456 015901. www.eoc.org.uk
Federation of Small Businesses, Sir Frank Whittle Way, Blackpool Business Park, Blackpool, Lancashire FY4 2FE. Tel: 01253 336000. Provides information on becoming a member. Web-site: www.fsb.org.uk/
Health and Safety Executive Information Line. Tel: 08701 545 500. Gives information and provides publications on a wide range of business health and safety issues. www.hse.gov.uk
Inland Revenue – general enquiries regarding tax matters, PAYE, expenses and benefits: call your local tax office for information. Check your local phone book under 'Inland Revenue'.
The Telecottage Association, WREN Telecottage, Stoneleigh Park, Warwickshire CV8 2RR. Tel: 02476 696986, www.tca.org.uk

Voluntary work

National Centre for Volunteering, www.volunteering.org.uk
TimeBank. Tel: 020 7927 8323, www.timebank.org.uk

Web-sites for women

These web-sites cover all sorts of issues relating to women, including jobs and careers:

www.femail.co.uk
www.ivillage.co.uk/workcareer
www.womenback2work.co.uk

Index